NURTURE

Connecting the Social, Emotional and Cognitive Needs of Children

Dr. Mattie Lee Solomon

iUniverse®

NURTURE
CONNECTING THE SOCIAL, EMOTIONAL AND COGNITIVE NEEDS OF CHILDREN

iUniverse books may be ordered through booksellers or by contacting:

iUniverse
1663 Liberty Drive
Bloomington, IN 47403
www.iuniverse.com
1-800-Authors (1-800-288-4677)

Because of the dynamic nature of the Internet, any web addresses or links contained in this book may have changed since publication and may no longer be valid. The views expressed in this work are solely those of the author and do not necessarily reflect the views of the publisher, and the publisher hereby disclaims any responsibility for them.

Any people depicted in stock imagery provided by Thinkstock are models, and such images are being used for illustrative purposes only. Certain stock imagery © Thinkstock.

ISBN: 978-1-5320-0856-6 (sc)
ISBN: 978-1-5320-0857-3 (e)

Library of Congress Control Number: 2016916708

Print information available on the last page.

iUniverse rev. date: 11/23/2016

NURTURE

Connecting the Social, Emotional, and Cognitive Needs of Children

My reflections of children are as beautiful flowers in a garden. An expert gardener knows that for plants to grow and flower to their full potential, they must be properly nurtured. Each variety of flower may have different needs, but their differences make the garden so beautiful … and so it is with children; they are each uniquely different and beautiful.

"The Lord watches over those who fear him, those who

rely on his unfailing love"—Psalm 33:18

To nurture a child is to love him.

Nurture is dedicated to all those who have been blessed with the

responsibility of caring for the children of this world.

Contents

Acknowledgments

The idea for *Nurture* was cultivated from reflections of my many observations of children as they interacted with the adults in their lives. My previous books afforded me the opportunity to document the perspectives of parents concerning their roles in the educational process of children, share real-life stories of those who revealed their personal childhood experiences, and observations of child-care workers' interactions with children. As a result, I acquired valuable information that enabled me to provide support and training for those who care for children.

I would like to acknowledge those whose passion for children led them to a career in child care and professional individuals whose dedication to the health and well-being of each child steered them to conduct research that answers the countless questions affecting how we nurture our most valuable asset—children.

Introduction

My reflections of children are as beautiful flowers in a garden. An expert gardener knows that for plants to grow and flower to its full potential, they must be properly nurtured. Each variety of flower may have different needs, but their differences make the garden so beautiful. *Nurture* is an action word. The dictionary gives these definitions: The act or process of promoting the development etc. of a child; something that nourishes; to feed and protect or support and encourage.

For example, the gardener (caregiver) must be willing to put the time and effort into nurturing the growth of each flower variety. To be successful, gardeners must dedicate themselves to learning about and caring for an array of plants and flowers.

I love roses; they are one of my favorite flowers. They come in many colors and varieties. I have tried many times to grow roses, but the experience has been very challenging. I first planted roses with a purple tint, but the rose bush did not grow. I tried another variety that was orange, but it soon died. Finally, I tried a red rose bush, which survived for two seasons and then became unproductive. I could not understand why I was not having success growing this beautiful flower that I loved.

It soon became apparent to me that I did not know what I was doing. I had to do some research to learn how to successfully grow roses. The American Rose Society (ARS) provides information by rosarians (experts on roses). From the information on their website, I found there were many things I needed to take into consideration to become successful in growing roses.

I also found research to be beneficial as I endeavor to gain knowledge and expertise pertaining to the developmental needs of children. I had the opportunity to visit many child-care facilities to observe interactions and relationships between adults and the children in their care. I obtained the perspectives of parents by visiting homes and meeting with them at restaurants or at their children's activities or sport events. The documentation of my observations of child-care facilities and conversations with parents allowed me to share my expertise in the field of early childhood education.

I have shared my perspectives in the four books I have written, which cover the following areas: the perspective of parents concerning the educational process of their children; parents' personal experiences and how they affect how they parent; a guide for child-care providers on guidance for young children (discipline); and nurturing ways to connect the social, emotional, and cognitive development of children. Some excerpts from my previous books are included in *Nurture*.

As a presenter and trainer of early childhood education students and workers, I support the premise that healthy adult relationships are essential in nurturing young children. My current service on the board of the Indiana Association for the Education of Young Children (IAEYC) as the chair of the Professional Development Committee gives me an opportunity to play a vital role in advising the professional-development needs of child-care workers and child-care providers.

Many resource websites, such as the National Association for the Education of Young Children (NAEYC), of which I am a member, provide research and articles by experts pertaining to young children.

Children encompass many diversities and cultures. They not only are beautiful, but they also are our most valuable asset. Nothing is more worthy of our investment.

Research shows that in order to create a nurturing experience for children, three areas of development—social, emotional, and cognitive—must be connected. I have found throughout my observations that most preschools have the appropriate cognitive curriculum but lose sight of the importance of guiding children socially and emotionally. For example, a child who is not taught how to self-regulate (emotional) or get along with his peers (social) will have a gap in his cognitive development that can manifest as discipline issues. Making the connection between these three areas of child development play a crucial role in how children understand and interact with the world around them.

Nurture, discusses each area of child development and merging them together to show how children's development is connected to all of their experiences and interactions with adults and peers.

Nurture goes further by revealing the importance of these developmental connections as they are defined, using the comparison of the healthy mind, body, and spirit of a child. Finally, steps for working together to create a nurturing preschool environment for children is demonstrated and shared.

Part 1

Nurturing the Social Development of Children

Part I

Nighting the special treatment of Children

Part 1

Nurturing the Social Development of Children

Children are all beautiful. Their differences come from genetics and the situations to which they are exposed, socially, emotionally, and cognitively. As they grow and develop, that exposure becomes the ground that nurtures or depletes them. It is vital to nurture children appropriately from infancy.

Crucial brain development happens in the early years (birth to three years) of a child's life. During this time, children learn how to express themselves and gain confidence and creativity. A nurturing learning environment engages children socially, emotionally, and cognitively.

1   The Role of Play

Playtime is one important aspect of nurturing children's social development, and its value cannot be underestimated. During play, children are exposed to many learning and developmentally necessary interactions with their peers. Nurturing guidance is crucial at playtime because children are developing in areas that prepare them for when they reach school age, the teen years, and adulthood.

The following is an excerpt from my book *Disciplining Someone Else's Children* (2015), which examines the role of play as it pertains to the development of young children.

> Understanding a child's individual developmental progress is important in order to understand, accept, or correct his/her behavior (as well as the response of the teacher). Remember, children have differences in temperament, development, and behavior.

> An important part of discipline is knowing whether to intervene or let children be children. Safety is the first priority, and danger needs immediate action. It is the responsibility of the child-care providers to teach children, directly or indirectly. This may mean stopping or redirecting a child's undesirable behavior for his/her safety or the safety of other children.

> During my visits to several child-care providers' facilities, I observed that many teachers faced challenging behaviors during

playtime. Often, the teacher's frustration could have been avoided by understanding what children are experiencing developmentally during play. A website article by Child Action Inc. titled "The Importance of Play" brought out that children's behavior in play develops in stages.

"Play allows children to explore new things at their own pace, master physical ability, learn new skills and figure things out in their own way."

During play with others, children learn leadership skills by directing the action or by following a leader. The following are common stages of play:

- Onlooker behavior: watching what other children are doing but not joining in the play

- Solitary play: playing alone without regard for others; being involved in independent activities, like art or playing with blocks or other materials

- Parallel activity: playing near others but not interacting, even when using the same play materials

- Associative play: playing in small groups with no definite rules or assigned roles

- Cooperative play: deciding to work together to complete a building project or pretend play with assigned roles for all of the members of the group of children

Learning to share is a process that takes several years to develop. Children will need proper adult supervision to master this skill. If children do not master this skill, their reactions could cause discipline concerns. The article by Child Action, also defined the following three stages of development in learning to share:

- First stage: children think everything is "mine."
- Second stage: children discover that some things belong to others.
- Third stage: children know they can lend a toy and get it back. Children are more likely to share when they see their toy come back to them and when other children share with their toys.

During play, children also increase their social competence and emotional maturity. Smilansky and Shefatya (1990) contend that school success largely depends on children's ability to interact positively with their peers and adults. Play is vital to children's social development.

Play supports emotional development by providing a way to express and cope with feelings (J. P. Isenberg and M. R. Jalongo, April 2014). The importance of play in children's lives is well documented. As children grow and change, play develops with them, according to a developmental sequence.

Playtime is a necessary learning environment for children. Teachers would be wise to use this time to teach children many valuable social skills. Some preschoolers may have tantrums. Their tantrums, however, should not be as severe as a two-year-old because they should be gaining more control over their emotions. They also display aggressive behavior but should be learning to use their words instead of using their impulses.

Teachers should be concerned when children exhibit behaviors that professionals consider to be outside of normal misbehavior such as psychological behaviors that impairs their ability to function. It is normal for preschoolers is to try to gain more independence. For example, they may argue and exercise their right to say *no*. Preschoolers also want to have the freedom of older children, while still craving attention like a baby. Some warning signs of abnormal behavior referred to on the American Academy of Pediatrics website, https://www.aap.org are:

- Difficulty managing emotional outbursts
- Difficulty managing impulses (such as physical aggression, verbal impulses)
- Behavior that does not respond to discipline

It is normal for children to continue to repeat misbehavior from time to time. They do this to see if the care provider will follow through with discipline. Abnormal behavior, however, also may include the following:

- Misbehavior that does not respond to appropriate disciplinary action
- Behavior that interferes with school and causes a child to fall behind academically; behavior that interferes with social interactions.

Rosarians say that one very important aspect to successfully growing roses is to be consistent with their care and nurturing. Consistency is an essential element in the social development of children as well.

2   Self-Image

Each child is a unique individual. Babies have their own personalities, likes and dislikes and, yes, characters. To support a healthy, positive self-image, babies need to be exposed to a consistent and loving environment. Loving relationships are key. Children learn to love by being loved. Getting to know the character of each baby means learning to recognize to what he or she responds, such as sounds and facial expressions.

My daughter was a sensitive baby. If I looked at her with a sad face, she would tear up, but my happy face made her smile. From toddler age to teenage years, she did not like to see me look unhappy or disappointed. Knowing her character helped me determine how to respond to her when she needed correction and support. For example, since my daughter was sensitive to my feelings and was hurt whenever she felt that I was disappointed in her, I realized that she was a child who did not need to be spanked. I could redirect and guide her without being physical.

Babies eyes open soon after birth, and from that point on, they watch their surroundings and especially caregivers (parents and guardians). From birth, they are developing a sense of self. Their surroundings and interactions will have a negative or positive effect on how they view themselves as children and into adulthood. Toddlers watch the reactions and responses they get from the things they do. They also view themselves by the way they are treated. Positive or negative caregivers play a role in molding the self-image of children.

In my book *What Did Your Parents Do to You*, I share how outside influences that are out of parents' control, such as bullying, peer pressure, and other adult contacts (teachers, relatives), also shape children and how they react to life. (I defined parents as anyone who is legally responsible for the care of a child and those with whom the child lives.)

I have heard many stories in the more than twenty years I've talked to parents about children as an educator, school principal, and parenting trainer. I find it interesting to hear parents reflect on their own childhoods when dealing with their children. Parents have told me how they hated certain things their parents did to them, but they ended up doing the same thing to their children.

Children's responses to interactions with their surroundings are unique. The influence on their character is equally unique. It is said that dysfunction has become acceptable in our society, so much so that it has been given labels and reenacted on television as entertainment. Sitcoms, cartoons, and reality television profile dysfunctional situations. There are also sitcoms that portray the dysfunctional relationship between teachers and children in a classroom situation as entertainment.

Webster's Dictionary defines dysfunctional as "impaired to function." Impaired is to "make worse; to diminish in quality, value, excellence, and strength; to deteriorate." This definition leaves me pondering what type of deteriorating effect dysfunction has on children.

A well-known pastor and author, in one of his sermons, discussed how painful it is to try to get in adulthood what you should have gotten as a child. Sometimes children have both a negative and positive relationship with their caregivers—the kind of negative, hurtful experience that leaves them feeling unloved, mixed with positive experiences that make them feel that their caregivers do care and love them. These mixed, inconsistent interactions can cause a lot of confusion in their childhood and even into their adult lives.

Can we stop the cycle of damaging the self-images of children? I discerned the following from many conversations with adults (who shared their stories in my book *What Did Your Parents Do to You*): when a child is abused or mistreated, he or she may grow up to abuse and hate. As adults, they may hate what they are doing but cannot change their behavior. They may not realize that they are reacting to what happened to them in the past. Many children who survive bad experiences never tell anyone what they went through.

As adults, some say they do not feel that anyone would understand or believe them. They internalize the experience, and let it define who they are.

It is very difficult for a child to understand how those who are supposed to love and keep them safe can do the opposite. When children who have been mistreated act negatively, they are misunderstood and are thought to be solely to blame. These actions include fighting in elementary school, drug and/or alcohol abuse in high school, and sexual abuse as an adult. Many of these actions are a result of having a poor self-image.

Oprah Winfrey, in her book *What I Know for Sure*, shared that some of the things she experienced as a youth caused her to feel unworthy, and healing the wounds of the past was huge but worthwhile. She wrote, "I know for sure that healing the wounds of the past is one of the biggest and worthwhile challenges of life. It's important to know when and how you were programmed, so you can change the program."

It is obvious that when a garden has not received proper nurturing, the appearance (image) of flowers in the garden is affected. Studies show that when children are not properly nurtured at school and/or at home, their self-images can be affected in a negative way. With positive nurturing, however, such as intervention, support, and love, it is possible for a negative self-image to be transformed.

3   Expression

Flowering plants flourish and blossom in the appropriate environment, which includes the right amount of sunshine, water, and care. Children flourish when nurtured in a safe, caring, and learning environment, where they are loved and respected. When children feel safe to express what they want and feel, they blossom from young children into teenagers and adults in a positive way.

As an artist, I enjoy watching children express themselves through artistic means, such as coloring, drawing, and writing. Through these processes, children develop communication skills and social expression. Social expression is a way to show the world who they are in ways that cannot be put into words.

I've read many articles written by psychology expert Kendra Cherry. In the article "What is Art, www.verywell (2016), she stated that as an expressive medium, art can be used to communicate, overcome stress (children can and do experience levels of stress), and explore different aspects of one's personality.

The American Art Therapy Association describes art therapy as a process that can enhance the mental and emotional well-being of individuals of all ages. Art is also described as a toddler's first visual language. As stated earlier, children express themselves during playtime. They also learn cooperation, relationship skills, and respect for others. Caregivers should allow children to express themselves freely during play, while keeping them safe and using playtime for teachable moments.

Give toddlers objects with which they can build using their imaginations. As they reach school age they, learn to build by following verbal or written instructions. This activity makes them aware of the importance of guidelines.

From birth, children express themselves in uniquely different ways as they connect to their surroundings. Babies respond to their surroundings before they are born. As babies, they see, feel, taste and begin to connect by responding in ways that become expressions of who they are. As we pay attention to their responses to stimuli, such as noises, tone of voice, and facial expressions of others, we get to know their likes and dislikes. For instance, my daughter would get very disturbed if she heard yelling. I used this as a cue when interacting with her.

As children connect to their surroundings, they learn to focus and have self-control. The reactions that babies have to stimuli and the way they express themselves is different for each child. Author and leading child development expert Ellen Galinsky shared information on how infants connect to their surroundings in her book *Mind in the Making.* She notes that if we adults could find ways to relate to what babies are doing, we could understand what they are experiencing. We can gain this understanding by paying attention to the positive and/or negative ways the baby reacts to stimulation; then we can respond in a nurturing way.

4   Learning to Trust

As a component of my inquiry into the relationship children have with their caregivers, I observed that preschool children learn best when teachers develop positive and caring relationships with them. The teacher who is nurturing gains the trust of children more instinctively. Research shows that children learn best in safe, trusting, learning environments and will respond positively when they receive age-appropriate, carefully planned guidance and assistance.

Age-appropriate strategies nurture children at each age and stage of development. Preschool children have begun to develop a level of understanding and brain readiness from their experiences, activities, and interactions. The following is a reflection taken from my book *Disciplining Someone Else's Children* (2015).

Developing a trusting relationship with preschool children is essential to their emotional and social growth. I also have discerned that it is just as important for child-care workers (director, teacher, teacher assist, etc.) to gain the trust of the children in their care as it for the children to trust their parents. Child-care workers have a responsibility for initiating and developing this trusting relationship.

A trusting relationship can be developed and maintained by providing children with opportunities, letting them know that they are cared for and safe, and by treating them with respect. The way to provide opportunities is by allowing them to do things that they want to do and not limit them. Let children try new things and new ways of doing things. It is the teacher's responsibility to keep them safe by monitoring and facilitating the activity. Allowing children to explore is a way to build trust.

I have observed that teachers who have created a safe learning environment in the classroom are most often more relaxed. They are comfortable with allowing children to make their own choices from the activities or workstations in the classroom, such as dramatic play or manipulative stations. This allows the children to have a sense that the teacher trusts them and that the teacher is willing to let them learn on their own.

As the teacher monitors the children, he or she has confidence that even if a child gets in trouble that this can be a healthy learning experience or maybe even a teachable moment. Children need and want to know that they are important. Children learn to trust when teachers let them know that they care about them, no matter what— even if they get in trouble.

When redirecting or stopping undesirable behavior, the teacher can demonstrate that he or she cares about the child by giving the child a task to do, such as letting the child be a helper for the day. This sends the message, "I do not care for your behavior, but I do care about you."

"Let yes mean yes and no mean no." I know you may have heard this saying before, but it is very important when communicating with young children. Being consistent with responses is the key. I find that preschool children will respond to expectations because they want to please. The rules should not change on a day-to-day basis, depending on the teacher's mood.

Children should know what to expect, even if they get into trouble.

When undesirable behavior has a consequence, the consequence should be communicated clearly and carried out. Yes, even carrying out a consequence builds trust. Consequences are to correct undesirable behavior, not "threats."

In the same way, promises should be kept. If, for example, the teacher makes a promise to give extra recess time or a treat to children who complete a task, the teacher should follow through with the promise. Breaking a promise can have a damaging effect on building a trusting relationship. I believe and have seen that when preschool children have a trusting relationship with their teachers, they bounce back easier and quicker from adverse and challenging situations.

It is imperative to the social emotional development of their children that parents support the efforts of their child-care providers to correct undesirable and disruptive behavior. They have to be on the same page to get appropriate results.

Young children need the help of loving parents and child-care providers to develop strong, secure, trusting, bonding relationships during the infant years through age three. If they develop correctly, the independence they want as toddlers will be balanced. When they become preschool age, however, they will continue to need the support of parents and their child-care provider to build more and more confidence and trust in themselves.

The social contact children have with adults also provides the stimulation and experience their brains need to develop in a healthy way. The love that is shown to children through the way they are touched can send positive, soothing messages that make them feel loved and special. This social growth is paired with emotional development as they gain resilience, self-regulation, and trusting relationships. Advances in brain research show how the brain continues to grow and develop after birth. It has been demonstrated that the growth of the brain is not only determined by genetics; it is also dependent upon the child's experiences. Interactions with other people and objects are vital for the growth of the brain, in the same way food nourishes the body. As stated earlier, as children grow and mature, their ability to become socially and emotionally healthy will be affected by the relationships they have.

While positive early experiences help the brain to develop well, negative experiences, such as neglect and abuse, can cause some genetically normal children to have mental disorders or to develop serious emotional problems. Supporting information found in the article "Facts for Life: Child Development & Early Learning Facts" brought to light that each time a child uses any one of the five senses a neural connection is made in the brain. As the child repeats using the senses, new connections are made that shape the way the child thinks, feels, behaves, and learns, which gives evidence that a close, nurturing relationship with child-care workers is a way to nourish a child's growing brain.

Part 2

Nurturing the Emotional Development of Children

Part 2

Nurturing the Positive Development of Children

Part 2

Nurturing the Emotional Development of Children

An American Rose Society rosarian stated that roses want to grow badly enough to overcome most deficiencies in techniques. Human beings will grow from infancy to toddlers; toddlers will grow to school age. How well they grow (develop) depends on how knowledgeable or unknowledgeable their caregivers (parents, guardians, child-care providers, teachers) are. Emotional development involves many learned behaviors. When children are infants, it is human nature for them to absorb their surroundings.

Children will model how they are treated and what they see and repeat what is heard. For this reason, caregivers must not be afraid to give and show love to children. Children need unconditional love.

The definition of unconditional love is affection without limits or conditions; complete love. The Bible says that God loves us unconditionally—what a wonderful gift. It is also said that children learn to love by being loved. Through my research for the book *What Did Your Parents Do to You*, I met many adults who grew up never knowing what it meant to be loved unconditionally. It is very difficult to share an experience with a child that you did not experience yourself.

Love is an important key to nurturing a child to be healthy emotionally. A child who is developing in a healthy way will have positive social and emotional responses to life through resilience, self-regulation, and forming relationships.

5   Resilience

Resurgence & Ecologist magazine chose a flower for the cover of their November–December 2009 issue to illustrate "resilience."

> Blossoms and flowers are resilient; they stand out there in the wind, in the rain, in the snow, in sunshine—day and night—unperturbed, undiminished. They are resilient because they are flexible and fragrant, pliable and pleasant, supple and soft, tender and tolerant, gentle, adaptable and light.

Bing dictionary define resilience as "speedy recovery from problems: the ability to recover quickly from setbacks. Elasticity: the ability of matter to spring back quickly into shape after being bent, stretched, or deformed."

Caregivers should be aware of the importance of teaching children to be resilient—to bounce back—and should not assume that resilience just happens. This ability is important to surviving in life. With resilience, individuals and communities are able to rebuild their lives, even after devastating tragedies.

During times of tragedy, adults are in survival mode, and resilience is not something that they think of with regard to children. Unintentionally, adults may not stop to make sure children learn from whatever has happened.

Children are not born with resilience; it develops as they grow up and gain better thinking and self-management skills and knowledge.

The factors that cause children to commit suicide differ slightly from their older counterparts. Depression can play a role, but among the youngest suicides, a predisposition to impulsiveness is just as important. Children who kill themselves often have a mood disorder, ADHD, or a "conduct disorder," which basically means antisocial behavior.

Living an in abusive household can lay the groundwork for suicidal behavior, and an incident like getting kicked out of school or a dying relative can trigger it. Bully-related suicide can be connected to any type of bullying, including physical bullying, emotional bullying, cyber-bullying, and "sexting" or circulating suggestive or nude photos or messages about a person.

A few years ago I read an article about a six-year-old boy who committed suicide because he was upset over his parents' divorce. Being resilient doesn't mean going through life without experiencing stress and pain. People feel grief, sadness, and a range of other emotions after adversity and loss. The road to resilience lies in working through the emotions and effects of stress and painful events.

What has happened that a child comes to the point where there is no hope? How can adults set an example of resilience for the children in their care? We cannot say, "They are young; they will get over whatever situation is causing them distress". Factors that contribute to resilience include close relationships with family and friends; a positive view of self; confidence in personal strengths and abilities; and the ability to manage strong feelings and impulses.

According to Edith H. Grothberg, the manner in which parents and other caregivers respond to situations serves as a model for children. The way they help a child to respond is important because their response will both promote and inhibit resilience. Many say that adults and children share some of the same indications of resilience, such as the ability to relate to other children and adults; the ability to bounce back after a negative interaction; courage; and laughter.

Child caregivers should know and look for signs of resilience in the children they have in their care so that they can provide teaching, support, and intervention. Resilience also plays a key role a child's ability to self-regulate.

6   Self-Regulation

Socially, children learn to respond and relate to their peers and adults in a healthy way. Emotionally, they learn to self-regulate and have self-control. Helping children develop self-regulation skills is similar to helping children learn to read and write. Nurturing teachers use a variety of strategies to connect that which children learn socially and emotionally to more complex skills and knowledge. Three teaching strategies found to be critical to children's development of self-regulation are modeling, using hints and cues, and gradually withdrawing adult support.

Self-regulation is clearly not an isolated skill. Children must translate what they experience into information they can use to regulate thoughts, emotions, and behaviors (Blair & Diamond 2008). For example, infants may translate the feel of a soothing touch and the sound of soft voices into cues that help them develop self-calming skills.

Toddlers and preschoolers begin to translate cues from adults—such as "Your turn is next"—into regulation that helps them inhibit urges to grab food or toys. They learn how long they must usually wait to be served food or to have a turn playing with a desired toy, rather than just grabbing them, which also helps them regulate emotional tension. Research show that emotional regulation has a connection with every aspect of a child's developmental well-being (Bell & Wolfe, 2014).

Self-regulation has been compared to using a thermostat because both are active, intentional processes. Setting a thermostat requires an intentional decision, and the device actively monitors environmental temperature. Similarly, self-regulation requires intentional decisions and active processes by the child.

Although children's behavior is regulated by many processes that function outside their awareness, researchers have found children's intentional self-regulation predicts school success (Zimmerman 1994). When provided with appropriate opportunities, young children can and do learn intentional self-regulation. Researchers found that planning helped children develop stronger self-regulation skills (Bodrova & Leong 2007).

Planning is an important part of self-regulation. As children develop, their regulatory skills become more sophisticated (Kopp 1982; Blair & Diamond 2008). Studies have sound that infants begin to regulate arousal and sensory-motor responses even before birth. An infant may suck her thumb after hearing a loud sound, indicating that she is regulating her response to the environment.

Toddlers start to inhibit responses and comply with adult caregivers. By age four, children exhibit more complex forms of self-regulation, such as anticipating appropriate responses and modifying their responses when circumstances are subtly different. For example, clapping is appropriate after someone speaks during sharing time at school but not while a teacher is giving directions.

Self-regulation skills develop gradually, so it is important that adults hold developmentally appropriate expectations for children's behavior. Adults create routines to help manage and guide children, and if these routines are consistent, they also help children self-regulate. Routines that are consistent involve activities that happen at about the same time and in the same way each day.

During my observations at several child-care facilities, I noticed that most of the teachers had a daily morning routine. It was during the morning routines that children appeared comfortable and displayed a sense of emotional security. Routines also provide an opportunity for the teacher to model behavior for children. By demonstrating appropriate behavior, teachers show children how to accomplish a task and use self-regulation skills needed to complete the task.

Child-care experts say that routines help children learn to trust that the adults in their lives will provide what the children need. This trust gives children the freedom to play, explore, and learn.

The social skills that children develop are important to their cognitive development. Children who develop positive social skills, such as self-regulation, transition more successfully at school age and reach academic achievement (Ladd, Birch 1996).

7   Trusting Relationships

As mentioned earlier, loving and caring relationships make the connections that babies need to get to know the world and their places in it. The way that young children are treated and the experiences they have, both positive and negative, form the reference they will use throughout the rest of their lives. Relationships guide children as they develop socially and emotionally, which includes the ability to play, communicate, learn, face challenges (resilience), and emotionally regulate (self-regulation).

Most importantly, children need trusting relationships to develop empathy, compassion, sharing, and an overall sense of well-being. Children must form secure relationships that give them the freedom to explore and learn if they are to thrive.

Children experience their world through the relationships and interactions they have with adults. It's important that these relationship be safe, stable, and nurturing. "Essentials for Childhood: Steps to Create Safe, Stable, Nurturing Relationships & Environments for All Children," published by the Center for Injury Prevention and Control (CDC) 2014, documented findings that confirm that three critical qualities that make a difference for children as they grow.

These three qualities also shape the development of children's physical, emotional, social, and cognitive development, which also will affect their health as adults. These qualities are as follows:

- Safety—the extent to which a child is free from fear and secure from physical or psychological harm within their social and physical environment

- Stability—the degree of predictability and consistency in a child's social, emotional, and physical environment

- Nurturing—the extent to which a parent or caregiver is available and able to sensitively and consistently respond to and meet the needs of the child

As a school administrator, I learned a great deal from the large Hispanic culture in one of schools I was assigned to serve. I did research to gain a better understanding of the Hispanic culture, which increased my awareness of how to better communicate with the parents and their children, and I was able to nurture the children in a more meaningful way. When caregivers show respect for a child's culture, they will gain trust from the parents and their children.

I also found that the type of relationship and interaction children have with adults is influenced by their culture. The culture in which children develop has a great influence on the way they respond to the world around them. Culture affects a child's daily routine, for instance, and basic beliefs and values. The way that a child's parents' culture displays love and compassion will affect the way that the child is nurtured, as well as the way the child is disciplined.

8   Guidance (Discipline)

Discipline is vital to providing a nurturing environment for children of all ages. A nurturing environment that is conducive to learning does not tolerate disruptive behavior. This guidance is used as a way to teach and is administered in a consistent, nurturing, and loving way.

Child-care providers should depend on their understanding of the social and emotional development of children to correct unwanted behavior. Child-care providers may use professional development tools, such as the book *Disciplining Someone Else's Children*, which I wrote in 2015 to provide guidance for prevention and intervention in this area of child development. The following is an excerpt from this book.

Strategies for disciplining young children have gained many descriptions, such as classroom management, setting limits, setting boundaries, redirection, teaching self-control, and teachable moments. The *Merriam-Webster Dictionary* defines discipline as control that is gained by requiring that rules or orders be obeyed and punishing bad behavior and a way of behaving that shows a willingness to obey rules or orders.

The discipline policies used by child-care providers should be clear and shared with parents. Parents have many questions and concerns about discipline, and there should be a collaboration with the child-care providers that influence actions taken at home to correct behavior. Child-care providers have shared with me that their efforts to correct unwanted behavior are unsuccessful when parents do not set the same expectations in the home

One alarming concern today is the suspensions and expulsions of young children from child-care facilities. Suspension is an extreme disciplinary action because the child is removed from the learning environment for a short or long period. Expulsions are used in some cases, meaning the child is removed permanently. Does this type of discipline work? In *Disciplining Someone Else's Children*, I shared an interview I conducted with a director of a child-care facility with over two hundred children. In the following, suspension of young children is the focus of my interview with the child-care facility director.

Interview with a Child-Care Facility Director

Me: Director Carey, what age group of children have you had to suspend from your child care?

Director: The youngest child was age two. Children are suspended mostly because of continual fighting with the other children or when we cannot get the parents to help with the situation. Some children bit when they fought with the other children. One of the discipline rules of our facility is three bites, and you are suspended.

We actually gave one child more than three chances to change her behavior. This child bit up to ten times. We suspended the child for two days.

Me: How did the parents react to the child being suspended?

Director: They were a little upset but not surprised because we gave them plenty of warnings concerning the child biting and fighting.

Me: Did the suspension change the child's behavior?

Director: No, not really. When the child came back, the biting and fighting continued. We realize that biting is an issue with some two-year-olds, but children who are three and still biting become a concern.

Me: Does suspension work, in your opinion?

Director: Suspension sometimes works. For example, one child hit a teacher and was throwing toys. The child was suspended for a day, came back, was calm for about a week, but then went through the same behavior and process of suspension again.

Me: As the director, what role do you play in the decision to suspend a child?

Director: In most cases, the teacher will call for me to come to get the child who is acting out of control in a classroom. I will get the child out of the room and take him or her to my office.

Parents are then called and given direction to come get the child immediately. About 80 percent of the parents will or can come immediately. Some of the children have to sit in my office to wait on them.

When children are out of control to the point that no redirection or discipline will correct or stop the behavior, parents are asked to take them home, most times for the day.

It is the extreme situations that causes the child to be suspended for longer periods, such as biting or throwing things at the teacher or other children.

Me: What is cause of children getting out of control?

Director: I have found that most children want to please their teacher. They act out when they have not bonded with the teacher or when they don't feel like the teacher cares about them.

When I go to the classroom to get a child that the teacher has called me to remove, the first thing I try to do is give the child a hug. I hug him and love on him and comfort him. The child will respond in a positive way because she trusts me. I can often get her to go back in the classroom without any other incident that day.

The child has gotten some loving from me and that settled him or her down. I try to be an example. Some teachers get it; some don't.

I have not seen evidence the suspensions really work. It seems to just relieve the teacher of the aggressiveness of a child who is out of control for whatever reason.

We will suspend children permanently if they are a danger to themselves or others. I love them all, and I do not like to suspend our children.

Reflection after the Interview with the Child-Care Director

It is my experience that most child-care directors use suspension as a last alternative to correct behavior. This action is usually taken to get the attention of parents and to make them aware of the seriousness of the problems they are having with a child. This action may also be used as an example to the other children that certain behavior will not be tolerated.

Whenever I ask child-care facility owners or directors to share their perspective on the suspension of young children, I first notice a facial expression that reveals a sense of dismay as they proceed to share the instances that led them to determine that suspension was necessary. I found that they are very much aware that children need to be in a safe learning environment and that suspending them may be taking them away from what they need.

They tell me that the safety needs of all the children in their care has to be taken into consideration. It is for this reason that they do what is necessary, and they hope that parents understand and that the children learn that they love them but certain behavior is not conductive to learning and will not be tolerated.

Disciplining young children requires clarification because of the damaging effects it can have, if not administered correctly. Some child-care providers clarify how they discipline by providing a discipline policy. The discipline policy is shared with child-care workers and parents.

The discipline policy clarifies the appropriate responses to misbehavior—those that should not be done under any circumstance and those that are acceptable.

After spending many hours in several child-care facilities, observing the interaction between the classroom teacher and the children, I found that teachers have developed the knowledge and skills to deliver age-appropriate curriculum much more easily than the skills needed to implement the strategies for dealing with a disruptive child.

The *Merriam-Webster Dictionary* defines prevention as the act or practice of stopping something bad from happening; the act of preventing or hindering. It defines intervention as intervening to become involved in something (such as a conflict) in order to have an influence on what happens.

I feel that child-care providers have one of the most important jobs in the world. On a daily basis, they are responsible for our world's most valuable asset—our children. They work in collaboration with parents as the child's first teacher.

Research has provided evidence that the first years leave a lasting impression on the lives of children. Cognitive, social, and emotional development of children is the focus of the daily routines and activities of child-care facilities. Discipline is a part of the social and emotional development of children and can hinder their progress if not dealt with appropriately.

To successfully nurture children in this area, teachers and other child-care workers should use strategies that answer the following questions:

- How do you prevent disruptive behavior that interrupts the learning of other children?
- How do you intervene to stop disruptive behavior from getting out of control and becoming damaging to the other children in your care?

Helping children develop in the area of discipline is crucial to their overall well-being. How can child-care providers be sure they are making the right choices when it comes to this area of child development? Disciplining someone else's children is part of a child-care teacher's daily responsibility and a necessary part of creating a safe learning environment for all children.

Keep in mind that that each child is unique and develops at his or her own rate. There are also mental, developmental, and exceptional-needs issues that may require additional specialized guidance.

During my visits to child-care facilities, I observed that many of the teachers had the tendency to use the same discipline actions over and over again, whether it worked previously or not. They seemed to do this during times when they allowed themselves to become frustrated. Some of the actions I observed teachers use are as follows:

- Threatening to take away an activity that they know the child enjoys (e.g., recess)

- Yelling out the child's name over and over

- Saying things that are meant to shame the child or make him or her feel guilty

- Involving the other children in the classroom by using the child as example of wrong or bad behavior

In the health article "It's Not Discipline—It's a Teachable Moment," author Tara Parker-Pope quoted Dr. Ginsburg's statement, "It's not about punishment. It's about teaching. That changes things."

When discipline is used as punishment, teachers lose the opportunity to teach.

Certain situations with children that escalate into a child's being disciplined (punished) could have been prevented. At each age and stage of development, children learn to manage their emotions and relationships. To learn to do this, they must experience many life events and situations. It is the responsibility of child-care providers to understand and nurture them through these situations.

Both "spoiled" and harshly disciplined children are at risk for emotional and behavioral problems. Being consistent in the approach or discipline strategy can change the course of the child's development. The children's emotional response is determined by their age and stage of development. Keeping this in mind, what might be seen as misbehaving may be a necessary teachable moment for the child.

An example would be a two-year-old who is upset or unhappy because a toy he or she favored was taken away (this is a normal response for a toddler). A caregiver who is aware of the age and stage of development of child would use this understanding to teach the child how to handle the emotion and how to move on (transition).

For more information and resources on developmentally appropriate practice (DAP) go to the National Association for the Education of Young Children website at naeyc.org/DAP.

Part 3

Nurturing the Cognitive Development of Children

Part 3

Identifying Abuse and Neglected Children

Part 3

Nurturing the Cognitive Development of Children

I describe a beautiful garden as one that contains many varieties of flowers—flowers of different shapes, colors, and fragrances. Each specimen of flower grows at specified rates. The gardener has to take into account the whole plant as it develops from a seed or bulb into what it was designed to be. In comparison, in order for a child to develop cognitively in the adequate way, the whole child has to be taken into account.

My studies revealed that children develop cognitively as they develop socially and emotionally. Part 3 will put into perspective how the social and emotional development of children play a vital role in connecting to children's cognitive needs (learning processes).

To nurture children to their full potentials, their individual uniqueness also must be taken into consideration. Two of these unique areas include character and level of mental readiness. Brain research shows that children are ready to learn specific cognitive skills at different ages and levels of mental development. For this reason, if learning is to take place, activities must be precise and appropriate and must accommodate the level at which children are mentally ready to learn.

As children grow and develop, they also reach milestones—the actions that most children able to do by a certain age, such as crawl or draw. Advances in brain research confirm that children began to learn the moment they are born. The first years of life impact the success they will experience at school age.

As described in the article "Memory and the Brain" on the website the Human Memory (www.human-memory.net/brain_neurons.html), early experiences that are nurturing create a brain with more neuron structures that determine intelligence and behavior.

Children grow tremendously in all three areas of development during three first three years of life. A newborn's brain is about 25 percent of its adult weight. By age three, the brain has produced billions of cells and hundreds of trillions of connections, or synapses, between these cells. The Human Memory website defines synapses as being the memory of the brain. The core component of the nervous system, in general, and the brain, in particular, is the neuron—a nerve cell, "the brain cells" of popular language. This important development of the brain demonstrates the need to understand how learning is stimulated in children.

9   How Children Learn

As stated earlier, studies show that children learn from the surroundings, actions, and reactions of other people, such as; parents, relatives, other children, and teachers. This learning from others comes during play and everyday experiences. Children also learn from verbal and nonverbal communication. Language and conversation (talking) is learned from listening and repeating what they hear. I find it fascinating that from birth children can learn more than one language.

Bruce Perry, MD, PhD, in his article "How Children Learn Language," stated, "In the first years of life children listen, practice, and learn."

He indicated that there is no genetic code that leads a child to speak English or Spanish or Japanese. Language is learned; humans are born with the ability to make up to forty different sounds, and, genetically, our brains can make associations between sounds and objects, actions, or ideals. Combined, these abilities allow the creation of language, and through this process, sound has meaning.

Research by Tamar Kushnir "Learning about How Children Learn," 2009 shed light on the ways that children learn through everyday experiences. Her findings show that children display psychological intuition. Children achieve this by observing the actions of other human beings and then by coming to a conclusion about the underlying reason they do what they do. She found that children also ascertain the motivations, desires, and preferences that are displayed during the actions of others.

Cognitive development is defined by the Centers for Disease Control and Prevention (CDC) as the learning process of memory, language, thinking, and reasoning. During the first years of life, babies develop bonds of love and trust with their parents and others. This takes place as part of their social and emotional development. The CDC has determined that the way in which babies are cuddled, held, and played with will set basis for how they will interact with their parents (guardians) and others.

I firmly believe that child-care providers are most effective when they use age-appropriate strategies in all areas of early learning. The NAEYC online resource describes developmentally appropriate practice (DAP) as appropriate teaching, grounded in research on how children develop and learn in effective early education. The NAEYC DAP approach involves teachers interacting with children at their age and stage of development. Accomplishing this goal will help each child meet challenges and increase levels of achievement and learning, as well as increase his or her potential.

10   Developmentally Appropriate Activities

Teachers and caregivers can consult many important resources and research materials when developing age appropriate activities. A child's age and stage of development should be taken into consideration when planning all activities which involves providing them with activities at a level that their brains are ready to process. For example; a two- or three-year-old is given an activity—to place the correct color blocks onto a sheet containing the same colors. As the child places the colors onto the sheet, he or she says the name of the color. An infant would not be given this activity.

Child development experts say that children should be challenged as their brains mature and are prepared to process new information. An example would be a three- or four-year-old who is taught not only how to pronounce the names of and recognize the colors but how to spell and identify items that come in each color during the same activity.

The "Nature, Nurture and Early Brain Development" publication by Sara Gable noted the following information, taken from the book *Creative Curriculum for Infants and Toddlers* (Dombro, Laura, Colker, Dodge & Trister, 1997), which brought out that caring for infants and toddlers is also about building connections through everyday routines and experiences. During the first three years of life, infants and toddlers look to their caregivers for answers to the following questions:

- Do people respond to me?

- Can I depend on other people when I need them?

- How should I behave?

- Do people enjoy being with me?

- What should I be afraid of?

- Is it safe for me to show how I feel?

Emotional expressions are used by children to communicate before they learn to talk. Research shows that a baby's positive or negative emotions and the child-care worker's sensitivity to him or her can help support early brain development; for example, a shared positive emotional expression between caregiver and infant, such as smiling and laughing, which engages the brain in a positive way and promotes a feeling of security in the child. Also, when expressions between the child and caregiver are accompanied by heavy emotions, such as sadness and crying, these are remembered and recalled (Dombro, Colker & Dodge, 1997).

Continual professional development prepares child-care workers, teachers and caregivers in this very important area of child development. Learning how the young brain is stimulated to learn as it grows supports the need for age-appropriate activities. Age-appropriate activities are fundamental for the healthy social, emotional, and cognitive growth of young children. As stated earlier, all of the interactions young children have with adults must be age-appropriate in order to be effective in encouraging them as they transition from one level and milestone to the next.

Part 4

Nurturing the Parent Connection

Part 4

Nurturing the Parent Connection

Just like gardeners, parents have different levels of knowledge, skills, and passion. A beautiful garden reflects the amount of passion, dedication, and nurturing the gardener is willing to invest. Children are a reflection of the nurturing they receive from the adults in their lives, especially parents. Parents are an important factor when it comes to nurturing the cognitive development of children. The following is an edited excerpt from *Missing Link?*, a book I penned a few years ago.

It contains parents' perspective on whether or not they felt linked (or connected) to the educational processes of their children.

I started *Missing Link?* by sharing my experience as a teenage parent, which gave me an opportunity to reflect on my personal involvement in the educational process of my child. Through interviews, many parents were willing to share their perspectives as well.

The interviews with parents from *Missing Link?* are shared as way to stimulate conversations with parents and encourage collaboration between them and educators. It is my intention that the reader will glean a better understanding of how parents feel about the educational process of their children and develop ways to connect and support them.

When I turned eighteen, I became the mother of a beautiful baby girl. I felt that I was prepared to be a mom because I knew how to change a baby's diaper and how to feed her. I was twenty-three when my daughter started kindergarten; I then realized that I did not know how to extend being a mom at home to being a parent who supported the educational process of my child at her school.

I did know that I loved my daughter and wanted the best for her, but I had not received any training or advice on how to become linked to this important part of her life. I now know that even though I did not know what to do, I was quietly being held accountable.

I came from generations of parents who kept everything to themselves, including how to support their children's education. This may have been because they could not pass on to us what had not been passed to them. When parents my age talked about their children, it was mostly about how to make them behave. The important thing for us was that our children did not embarrass us in public. My daughter is now grown with a child of her own, and we have many discussions about the challenges I faced as a parent during her educational process.

As a teacher and school administrator, I had many opportunities to have discussions with parents concerning their role in the education of their children. Although I did not document those conversations, I knew how important they were. The discussions provided important insight into how their personal circumstances and challenges in life affected the link they had (or did not have) with the education of their children.

After taking an early retirement from school administration, I wanted to continue to dialogue with parents. I feel that it is important for parents to have an avenue to discuss how they feel and to share their perspectives with other parents and educators. Writing *Missing Link?* provided this avenue.

The parents interviewed in *Missing Link?* were not parents with whom I had contact as a teacher or school principal. They were parents who accepted an invitation to have a discussion of their perspectives concerning their children's education. I gained contact with these parents during various life situations, or they were referred to me informally. One-on-one interviews and/or small group discussions were not set about methodically.

My goal was to serve as an objective observer, not to advance an opinion but to collect feedback.

Parents interviewed were of all age groups and social and economic status. There were also many guardians who were in the role of parents of school-age children. These guardians might have been relatives who had guardianship of children in school, such as grandparents, uncles, aunts, and siblings who were thrust into the role of parents. In *Missing Link?*, all who had the responsibility of raising school-age children were called parents.

When it comes to the challenges parents face, parents explain their experiences the best. It is important that parents communicate with each other as well as with those who are linked to their children's social and academic development. Raising children is a journey best not traveled alone. The mistakes can be costly and sometimes irreversible.

What happens in the home has a great deal to do with the way a child views the outside world and society.

Research shows that what happens in the home also has a direct effect on the way a child responds to his or her environment. It is for this reason that the viewpoint of the parent has to be taken seriously. The perspective of the parent is valuable when answering the question, "What can educators do to improve student achievement?"

How parents feel about their children's education has to be articulated before we can take the necessary steps to involve them. The responsibility to develop children socially, emotionally, and academically cannot be one-sided, and passing the blame will not solve this dilemma.

Are parents the missing link to their children's social and academic progress? After conducting one-on-one interviews with parents and guardians, I found that parents had strong viewpoints, but some did not know how to articulate their feelings. This may have been because they had never been asked to have a conversation about their perspectives. For this reason, I used limited quotes in *Missing Link?*

Information concerning the perspectives of parents and what they value has to come from parents. There cannot be speculation about how parents feel because parents' views sometimes differ from those of the people educating their children. We have to meet them where they are in life.

As stated earlier, I decided to write *Missing Link?* as an avenue to more discussions with parents and to get a deeper understanding and insight about how they felt about the educational process of their children. This was not an attempt to answer questions for the reader; instead, it was an attempt to share parents' perspectives about how their children are being educated and their role in that process.

When I was asked to complete a survey from my child's school, my responses to the survey questions were mostly influenced by what my daughter perceived as a good or bad experience at school. All I had to go on were the stories that she would share with me about her day.

The many discussions I had with parents was an attempt to get parents to go beyond what they heard from their children. They were challenged to describe their feelings based on their personal experiences and interactions with the school. As a school administrator, I was faced with the dilemma of how to get parents involved when, in fact, many parents may have felt that they *were* involved.

The following chapters are the result of discussions I had with parents on several topics concerning parents' perspective about their connection to children's education. First, we will discuss the parents' answers to the question "Do you feel that parents are missing in the educational process of their children?" Next we will reveal the following discussions concerning why schools have a hard time getting parents linked to their children's education.

Discussions included topics such as empowering parents, who is responsible when a child fails in school, and what the responsibilities of parents are concerning the schooling of their children.

Missing Link? provides a better understanding of how parents feel about the role they play as a link in the chain of their children's social, emotional, and academic success. The chain of social and academic success for children has many links: parents, school, community, and church. All of the links have to be present and strong. If there is a weak or missing link, the child's chance for success is in jeopardy.

11   Parent Link (Missing Link?)

Do parents view their involvement in the educational process of their children the same way educators do? If not, does this difference in viewpoint cause educators to perceive parents as missing in the educational process? Parents discussed these observations and many other matters related to the factors that affect how parents view their children's educational process and how their view of these issues affects their children's views.

Other issues found to disconnect or link parents to their children's education are income status, educational level, and generational issues in families.

Parents openly discussed with me some of the reasons they feel they are missing in their children's education. One major reason was that parents may not know what to do or how to help.

A parent of two children in elementary school stated,

"Yes, parents are missing. If they don't have an education and the benefits that come with being educated, how can they encourage their children?"

Other than showing up for the Parent-Teacher Organization meetings, some parents do not know the next step. Parents felt that it's hard to be a part of their children's educational process if they don't know anything about it. They also felt that parents have not been taught how to support their children's education and have no idea what their role should be at school.

Most moms and dads will make an effort to show up at ball games and even to see their child perform in a play or sing in the school choir. Parents perceived that parents were missing except for these types of activities. They felt that the schools should schedule parent training before or after school plays, ball games, or other activities their children are involved in.

Are children who have both the mother and father present in the home at an advantage because the parents can support each other? When asked this question, parents said that this is not always true.

A mother of four said that when it comes to their children's education, her husband is missing.

"Because his mother was a single mom, he watched her do everything concerning her kids, and he feels that I should as well. So I have to take up the responsibility of making sure one of us stays connected to what is going on with our children's education."

Another parent stated that his mother valued education, but his father did not; he believed in hard work and was street-smart.

"He was not educated but told us that we had to finish high school, and we were afraid not to finish high school."

But when he did finish, his father was not at his graduation. This experience left him with a mixed message from his parents. He revealed that parents have to be the ones to push the child. He also shared that one of his children has a learning challenge, and so he is more lax with him concerning his school assignments than he is with his daughter, and his daughter became angry with him because he pushed her and not her brother.

He said that maybe he needed to take another look at how he is handling this situation.

"I don't want to send mixed messages about the importance of education to my children the way my parents did to my sisters, brothers, and me."

Knowing what is going on in the educational system is a challenge for some parents. As one parent stated,

"Education is always changing, upgrading, or evolving. Keeping up with the educational system seems to be a problem for many parents. They feel intimidated and do not always discuss this issue with the school."

One area in which they feel school districts have upgraded or evolved is the way they communicate with parents. Parents are contacted by an automated telephone system. A recorded message is sent out by the school to give information about events and school closings. Although the parents said they do not have a problem with this method of communication, some felt that it has taken away from the need to have a personal relationship with the school.

A teacher said during the interview that she felt her students' parents were linked with the school because they communicated with her on daily basis by e-mail, the school's website, in the car when they picked up the students, and when they signed off on journals brought home by the students. Her school provided laptop computers for parents to use, and the principal did home visits to help the parents set up the computers. She stated that as a parent, she felt that communication was the key and that using technology to communicate was one way to do it, and she was okay with it.

A parent who was also an elementary-school worker found that parents were uninvolved or missing in their children's education, and she shared the reason she felt this way.

"There is a vicious cycle of parents who are uneducated, and education is not important in the family."

Is it true that low-income parents do not have high expectations for their children's education? One parent explained how she felt in the following remarks:

"I don't believe that income is the determining factor in how parents view their children's education. To generally say that low-income parents don't hold high expectations is untrue. I myself was raised by a single parent who, at a particular time, was on welfare. Education was a high priority for our family. All of us (my two siblings and I) have college degrees. Two of us have graduate degrees. Low income/poverty does not equal failure. High expectations lead to higher achievement."

A parent who has a nine-year-old son in elementary school felt that there was a difference in how low-income and high-income parents viewed their children's education. This parent said,

"Parents who have a high income usually are educated or have worked really hard to get where they are. Therefore, they pass on to their children the knowledge and experience it takes to be successful. Those parents understand the value of education and that education is an investment. They also position their children to receive the knowledge and experience that it will take to be successful.

For example, they put their children in good schools, in great programs and activities. In contrast, parents who have low incomes most often depend on federal assistance or work in low-paying jobs. They may not have experienced enough success in their own education or the workplace to pass on these skills/values to their children.

Therefore, they value money more than education because money is tangible and is felt when it's scarce."

The perception of a parent who has a child in high school is that parents need to invest in their children's education. This parent said,

"You would think low-income parents would care more so that their children would make a better life for themselves and end the generational poverty. However, they don't care as much because they are living in survival mode. They are just trying to get their basic needs met. High-income parents know that it is possible to attain goals and hold their children to a higher standard. Higher-income parents send their kids to private schools. They are more financially invested in their children's future."

No matter what the circumstances are for the families, parents perceive that it is about holding someone accountable. Parents also shared that in certain aspects, the parents are missing. Nearly all of the parents I spoke with felt that parents with low incomes don't understand the power of influence they have on their children and on the educational system.

One teacher and parent of a child in middle school felt that parents should speak up.

"They are often too quiet on important educational issues involving their children. They may relate their income to the value of their vote. They also are not visible in our schools."

Parents also felt that, like low-income parents, parents with high incomes are not very visible because they have time-consuming jobs, but they are not quiet on educational issues and speak out loudly. They want the best for their children because they feel they make a big contribution through their taxes.

One parent had the following perspective:

"I think that all family situations are different. There are parents of low and high income levels who are not linked to the educational process of their children, and the same can be said for those who are linked. It depends on whether or not they value education."

Does the parent's need to be linked with his or her child's school lessen after elementary school? Parents said that their child's elementary school years were more crucial, but once the child is in middle school, there is more concern about his behavior because he goes through serious hormonal changes, and most children do not have control over their emotions. One parent imparted the following:

"I don't know if it is less. I think that it depends on how much the child is interested in school and whether or not the child has behavior issues. I have three boys, and they are good kids. I don't have to check on them as much as when they were in elementary school. One of my sons, who is in the tenth grade, has English and reading problems, so I do check with his teachers concerning his progress. I also do my part at home with him by having him read and write about what he read, and I check it and make the reading assignment a part of his allowance."

Parents revealed the importance of transitioning children slowly because once they leave the elementary level, changing the amount of pampering and attention would affect them in a negative way, and they might interpret this to mean that the parents no longer care. Parents are sometimes missing after elementary school; they feel that they do not need to be there in the same way. However, some parents felt that this was a mistake because even when children are older, they need just as much attention to stay on track—sometimes more.

Parent-teacher communication is even more important because the parent and teacher should work together to solve any issues that keep the child from being successful in school, including correcting the child's behavior.

One mother gave the following input:

"As children grow up, we parents teach them to be more independent and to start taking more responsibility for their schoolwork. My son works hard and tries to stay out of trouble because he knows that if he doesn't, I will be at the school. To boys, it's as uncool to have Mom show up at school when you are thirteen as it is when you are five or six."

Another parent felt that as the child gets older, there are fewer learning activities that require parents to be engaged at home.

"In elementary school, the child needs or requires more help with homework, projects, and other learning activities. As the child gets older, parents perceive less time is needed in this manner. As a parent, it seems to me that communication from the teacher to the parent declines as well. My daughter is in the tenth grade. Out of all of her teachers, I only receive communication regarding her progress from two. Even these are not very regular. When I attended the parent/ teacher conference, only one teacher, the dance instructor, gave me very tangible ways to help my daughter at home."

A parent of a seventeen-year-old daughter felt that parents are linked to children's educational process in elementary school more because they feel their children are still dependent on them for security.

"In elementary, they are doing a lot of milestone things, such as their first play and first musical. As children get older, parents tend to loosen the grip more and give them more independence. Their education is just as important, but we feel that we have established them with the school routine and instilled some of the basic values, so we don't have to be at the school once a week anymore."

One educator and parent described how she is on both sides of the fence. "Often I see myself in the parents' shoes. I feel parents work so hard to provide their children with the necessities that they rely heavily on the teacher for feedback. Since my job required so much of my time, it was hard to find time to visit or check up on my son.

As an educator, I always encourage parents to visit my class so they can see what goes on and how their children respond to my teaching. I recognized I had to start eating my own words. My argument was that my son is a good student; however, I realized that he valued positive feedback from me, his parent, way more than his teacher. I began to see him responding better to me visiting his class, just to hang out, than coming to talk to his teacher just when he was in trouble or for parent/teacher conferences. My presence in his classroom has made a big difference. My son is not a bad student, but he loves to see me in the class."

In the next chapter, parents share their perspectives concerning getting linked to their children's educational process. They discuss things that did and did not link them effectively and why.

12   Getting Parents Linked

Some parents feel they are so caught up with everyday life that they don't have time to engage in their children's education. Low-income parents are concerned with providing the basic needs of their children—and even that can be overwhelming.

However, being preoccupied with life situations and circumstances is not only an issue with low-income parents. Many parents felt preoccupied with some aspect of life, such as paying bills, job pressures, and health issues.

Parents also shared that being busy with other children and time restraints kept some of them from being linked to what is going on with each of their children's education. Other parents said that no matter what, parents should make time to be involved in every aspect of their children's lives, and they shared why they feel this is important.

A police officer and parent of a fourteen- and seventeen-year-old stated that he and his wife have always been involved through all grade levels of their children's education. An example he gave of their teamwork was when his daughter was accepted into the college of her choice. He and his wife went to every meeting and college event with her.

He also said,

"We work as a team. My wife and I saw kids being dropped off by their parents and noticed that some parents chose to let them do things on their own. I feel that it is important for the school and the staff to know that the parents are involved, and the parents should have high expectations for not only the child but for the school."

A father of four children felt that I needed to know a little about his background to fully understand his perspective on his children's education and his role in it. His feelings were tied to how his parents felt about education, and the link was broken when he and his nine siblings were in school. He has tried to repair the damage with his children.

This parent of four shared that his family was poor; his mother had a sixth-grade education, and his father had none. His mother taught his father how to write his name. He himself could do math in his head, and because he had a photographic memory, people thought that he could read. When he was little, his mother would help him read. She would also help him with words he could not pronounce, but as he got older, and she had a total of nine children, she did not have time to spend with him.

Despite the fact that he made straight "A's" in school, his teachers thought that he was having academic problems. He suspected that they did not recognize his academic success because they were focused on his family's poverty condition. He knew that his family did not have many of the necessities of life. The school fed them with leftover food from the cafeteria. He and his sibling had bad teeth and few clothes and because of this, the school staff thought he was an academic special-needs student.

"They thought that I could not learn because my family was poor."

Because the teachers were mostly young white teachers, he thought that they did not know anything about his culture and that although they tried to help feed his family, they had not been taught how to connect his parents to their children's education.

Parents were not sure what type of training, if any, the schools provided for teachers concerning parents but felt that the parents should be included in the training. They mostly were contacted by the school when children misbehaved or got hurt. During teacher meetings, the teachers took the lead in the conversation, and the parents were not asked what type of support they needed.

One parent stated,

"During parent/teacher conferences, they tell us why they feel the child is passing or failing. In most cases, the child is either completing his classwork and homework, or he is not."

Several parents said that they felt frustrated when they sometimes could not help with homework because they did not understand it themselves. They were embarrassed to tell the teacher that they did not have the knowledge to help with school assignments.

Does how parents feel about education affect how their children view education?

A father of a high school student replied,

"That is huge! Parents have to show that they value education by talking to their child about the importance of good grades and going to college. My wife and I always talk to our children about college. We let them know that there are no ifs, ands, or buts. They are going to college. We set the bar by being linked to their educational process. We also reward them when they do well with grades and citizenship."

Another parent's perspective:

"If parents feel education is important, they will instill those values in their children. Also, they will be more involved in assisting their child with homework and making sure that he attends school regularly.

I think it is imperative that parents are active in their child's education and lead by example."

A fifty-seven-year-old mother of three grown children, who is currently in school to complete her high school education, stated that she promised her grandchildren that she would get her diploma. She shared the following:

"My parents were uneducated, and of my three children, only one completed high school. I feel that I was affected by my parents' not finishing school, and my not finishing was passed on to my children. I am hoping that my going to back school now will make a difference to my grandchildren."

In the past, she said, she always could get a job. Some years ago, she worked in a factory for ten years and made what she felt was good money. At the present time, however, she couldn't get a job. She felt this was not because of her age but because she didn't have a high school diploma.

Parents shared that some parents just don't realize how important parent involvement is. They are consumed with their lives and problems, and they overlook the children's education. Parents also felt there was a lack of resources for the parents.

Does it sound like parents have many explanations for why they are not linked with their children's education? When asked if there are any good reasons not to know what is going on with their children, all to whom I spoke said no. They realized that parents need to find a way to balance things out.

Parents admit that they need help—for example, the schools could offer classes for parents, such as in budgeting finances and time management. They acknowledged that some parents need to learn parenting skills and that parenting skills consist of more than learning about academics and how to read test scores.

One parent said that she was frustrated.

"When the state test ISTEP is given at my child's school, they schedule a time to discuss the results with parents. I understand the importance of ISTEP but feel that I cannot do anything to help after the fact."

As stated earlier, the parents' frame of mind and focus is reflected onto their children. The children bring to school with them each day whatever their parents are going through at home. A state police officer and parent of two school-aged children stated,

"Parents who set higher educational standards for their children usually have high-achieving students who have education as a top priority. Parent satisfaction with the school also affects the children and how they feel about education. If a parent is highly satisfied, it will manifest in the child's performance and behavior in a positive way."

In order to create an effective parent and school connection, one parent felt there is a need to feel welcome when they visit the school.

"The schools should make the parents feel that they care about them and what they go through and give them the support they need."

Parents perceived that being made to feel welcome in the school would replace the occasional feelings that they are being blamed and not understood. One parent stated that when she spoke to the school about her child's failing grades, she felt they couldn't care less about her, and she began to shut down and feel helpless and overpowered in the situation.

Another parent who felt very welcome at her children's school stated,

"The principal and teachers are good at keeping me informed. They return my phone calls, and when I visit the school, they call me by name, and they know my child's name."

Being linked with their children's education was also important to parents because they felt that this meant knowing their child's teacher, school policies and politics, and volunteering when they could so that they could meet other parents.

According to a parent of a college student, parents should make themselves known in their child's school.

"You know you are linked when important people in the school (e.g., principal, teachers, and counselors) can put your face with your name. This happens when you participate in activities, such as visiting the classroom, helping with homework, and going to parent/teacher conferences."

Other activities parents mentioned were reading to their children's class and being a member of parent groups. Parents also believe that being linked means that parents need to know who their children are and what they are involved in. This means taking the time to listen and learn their interests. Sometimes it means pushing the issue until communication happens.

Parents confirmed that they should be helping children be successful in getting an education, and when they are involved, their children appreciate and know that they care about them.

Most important, it lets their children know that the parents support their education, sport events, or whatever they are doing. One parent said,

"If we as parents don't care, our children will be affected by our attitude and will develop a negative attitude toward school and sometimes even life. It is up to the home to keep children motivated. In the school setting, parent involvement should be that of the observer. The school system should be set up to thoroughly educate the child, and reinforcement should happen at home."

It is crucial for parents to realize that the link with their children's education also has an effect on their social and emotional well-being. Parents felt that this is important because it is directly related to how successful children are in all areas of their lives.

They also believed that for some parents, education was not a priority, for various reasons. Therefore, their participation in their children's education is lacking. For single parents, this may be because they work and are unable to make parent-teacher meetings or other activities that are usually set during the school day or before they get off work. As stated earlier, some parents, single or otherwise, are not aware of how to best be involved and support education at home.

One single dad said that when his two-year-old daughter attends school, he will be her first teacher. He feels that he sets the example of what she can expect out of life.

"I am her protector, and I will be involved from the beginning with her education. She will be aware of my presence, even when I am not there, because she will know that I may come to the school at any time. Some students are not focused, so they are lost. It is the parents' responsibility to help their children stay focused."

Another single parent who is preparing his son for preschool, felt that parents need to monitor what their children are being taught.

"Ever since he was six months old, I have said his ABCs with him every day. I know there are toys that will do this, but I feel that it is important for me to do it. My parents read to us, and Mom did not allow anyone to use baby talk when they were talking to her children. I feel that parents need to make the time needed to monitor what their children are being taught and spend productive time with them."

Being linked to children's education through knowledge and communication is powerful. The discussions in the following chapter will attest to what parents feel would empower them and why they need to be empowered concerning their children's education.

13   Empowering Parents

For decades, educators across America and the world have researched the answer to the question, "How can we improve parental involvement?" The answer has been linked to student academic success, discipline, and attendance issues.

I asked parents what they can do to empower themselves to be a positive link in the educational process of their children. Many parents felt parents should ask themselves, "If we do not get involved with our children, why should we expect the schools to take up our issues?"

The next discussion began with an explanation of being *empowered* as a parent. Empowerment means more than just being involved with school programs, such as athletics. Being empowered means that the parents know how to effect the necessary changes and demands that will influence the educational process of their children and ensure that effective academic and social developmental strategies are being implemented in the school.

One of the things parents felt was necessary was that there should be more conversations by schools with parents about how parents feel about their children's education and that schools should empower parents to educate and evaluate their children. Steps should be taken to bridge the gap of communication by understanding what type of communication is important to parents and not assume that parents don't care because they don't come to the school or call frequently.

Many of the parents I spoke with felt communication was one way they could be empowered. All forms of communication, such as calls, letters, e-mails, and Internet, would be helpful. Effective, consistent, and informative communication is the key.

A parent who felt that parents should not be surprised when a child bring home a bad report card also stated,

"There should be communication with the parent at the first sign of failure so that the problem can be identified and corrected, whether it is a home or school issue."

Another parent shared that communication is powerful.

"I think the schools just need to stay in constant communication with the parents. I like the web grades, where you can check your child's progress at any moment. I like the automated calls I receive when my child misses class. I also think that in high school, the school counselor should meet with the parents and a student to discuss the student's educational progress; this type of communication is powerful."

The perspective of parents is that they should be educated on the positive results of their involvement. Parents have different means, abilities, and needs; the school can create classes for the parent based on this information. The school should also have strict rules for students and parents. Parents agree that there should be consequences not only for students who break the rules but for parents as well.

They felt that some parents may have to break the generational habits of their parents and grandparents, who were not involved in their children's education, and that maybe the church could also be the link for spiritual guidance and support.

One grandmother who is the guardian of her daughter's school-age children said,

"If there are no past role models for parents in their family, they do not know what it is to be empowered to support their children's education. They have not had an example of how to communicate effectively with the school, and this can be intimidating and cause the link to be broken or never happen."

I invited a twenty-year-old guardian to have a discussion with me concerning her perspectives. This young adult has taken over guardianship of her sister's teenage daughter. She now has the legal responsibility of a parent for her niece's health, security, and education. During our discussion concerning empowering parents, she shared that her niece's school does not take her wanting to be involved in her educational process seriously.

She said that her relationship with the school started out with a lack of communication from the teachers, but it soon got better when she started showing up at the school regularly. She also shared the following,

"When you are having a grown-up life while people see others your age partying, it is hard for them to take your role as a concerned parent to a teenager seriously. I know I am a parent, and I need to have the same power that other parents have, because I influence my niece's dreams and visions the same way they do for their children. I have high expectations for my niece."

This guardian said there was a problem when she discovered that her expectations of educational issues were different from those of her niece's biological mother and her family. She felt that when one becomes the guardian of an older child and you do not know that child's history you may be unprepared to make the necessary decisions concerning her education and other issues.

She added,

"My niece had been told that she was doing well in school. I found that 'doing well' to her mother and other members of my family was a 2.0 GPA and issues with fighting the other students when things did not go her way. I not only need to be empowered by the school but also by my family if I am going to turn this young lady around. No one has truly sat down with me and wanted to know what I am going through. No one knows the sacrifice you make with a child; they only see the product."

One parent compared parents of the fifties, sixties, and seventies to modern parents. He felt that today's parents are disconnected. He also felt that the disconnection may have happened because "the neighborhoods have changed," and the black family he knew has changed.

"We have turned away from being a spiritual group of people and have allowed the media to dictate how we bring up our children. During my parents' day, there were partnerships with families and schools. The school knew that the family would discipline and do their part, but today's modern-day parents expect the school to be both parent and instructor, and they do not see anything wrong with it. Black educated people moving out of their neighborhoods could also be a cause, because the children do not see examples of all the different professions that people who look like them and come from the same place are involved in."

A parent who has three children in school, one at each grade level— elementary, middle school, and high school—felt that parents are empowered by getting to know their children's teachers, counselors, and coaches.

They should read the information the school sends home and ask questions of the school and their children. She also shared that parents cannot be lazy when it comes to the hard work it takes to make sure their children are getting the proper education. She concluded,

"If parents teach their children to respect authority, work hard, and value education, the children will model that. If a parent is lazy and apathetic, children will model that as well."

When asked about how they, as parents, could be empowered, two parents' perspectives were as follows:

"The more I know about my son's teachers and how they operate their classrooms, the more I am empowered. I like to know his/her teaching methods, his/her expectations for my child, and how my son responds to him/her. I learn these things by visiting the classroom, communicating often with his teachers, and communicating with my son.

I also like to know about the school's performance as a whole, what programs they offer, and the type of diversity of the staff. Knowledge is power, so the more I know about the teacher, the school, and the school district, the more it empowers me to be involved in my son's education. Parents have more power of influence then they know."

The other parent felt that whether they value education or not, the lack of involvement will have a negative effect on their children, but when they are involved, they have a positive effect. They teach their children principles, such as diligence, a good work ethic, effort, consistency, and that education is an investment worth more than fast cash. They do this by making sure their children are on top of things, such as turning in assignments on time and completing homework. They read material to children, have children read to them, and make learning fun. She said,

"When parents don't get involved, then children don't receive those important principles, and the effects spill over into adulthood. Those children often have a difficult time holding jobs and paying bills on time and usually depend on federal assistance."

A father of five children—two grown, two in college, and one on the way to college—felt that a parent has to want to be empowered.

"The empowerment comes from whatever the parents' desires are; if the parents want to be involved, they will go to the meetings, activities, and school events. In other words, parents empower themselves. When they step away, they give all the decisions about their child to the school, which may not be a good thing."

Parents perceived that it is powerful to just show up and be seen at the school, so the school knows they are caring parents. The parent shared,

"The schools need to know that they want to be a part of the educational process in a positive way and are not there to call the teacher a liar and cuss administration. I feel that parents should go to the school to be supportive. Parents are empowered by being there."

Parents gave many reasons for not being there for their children. However, they agreed that all stakeholders are responsible when a child fails. Most parents agreed that the utmost responsibility for the success of the children belongs to them. The next chapter will give insight into this important discussion.

14   Responsibilities

Whose fault is it when a child fails in school? Parents feel that the school, community, home, church—all the stakeholders—and the child each play a role in the child's success and that each must be held accountable when he fails. During our discussions, parents believed that they needed to be responsible for their children's education. Three of the parents' perspectives concerning this issue are as follows:

"Teachers do the educating, but it is on the parents to make sure the education is being effective for their children."

"Discipline at home is important because if the parents cannot control the child at home and make him do his homework, then what chance does the school have in the classroom?"

"Whatever the parents' value, the children will value, because parents are the only example some of them see. I am an educator, so I lead by example so that my children will value education. They were not given a choice as to whether or not they are going to college. … I told them, 'You may not want to go to college, but you are going from here.' I feel that it is my responsibility to enforce this value in them and not let them drift through life."

When it pertains to children, responsibility comes in many forms. One parent felt that discouraging and negative words that are spoken to a child can have a lasting, devastating effect. She felt that when teachers prejudge a child's social and economic environment, this judgment can be responsible for a student having a failing attitude.

This parent shared a situation involving a high school counselor who told a student who wanted to be a doctor that she could not be because there were no doctors in her family. She felt this remark discouraged the young lady and was responsible for the student's decision to drop out of school. She stated,

"I feel that everyone who has connection with the student should feel some responsibility for her success. Words are powerful."

One parent said,

"In a broad sense, there is often a correlation between the level of education and income. I think that when it is a generational thing, such as generational poverty, it is hard to break, but no matter what your economic situation is, the family is still responsible for the success or failure of its children. They will need more support, but they also have a responsibility to seek out the support they need."

Meeting the needs of her three children is a challenge for one parent. This parent expressed her need by saying,

"It would be very helpful for teachers to provide parents with information on how they can engage in learning activities with their child in the home, using everyday situations. They can communicate this through e-mail, newsletters, etc. Parents should also initiate these discussions with their teachers.

Perhaps a return to discussions on how parents can best be involved in their children's education is in order. It is the responsibility of parents to continue to inquire of their children about their school day, review their homework, look at their assignments and textbooks, and use teachable moments to relate everyday life to what their children are learning in school."

A parent of a child diagnosed with attention deficit hyperactive disorder (ADHD) commented that she asked her son's school for help with her child because she did not know what to do or how to handle a child with ADHD. The school was not able to provide her with assistance. She feels that schools should be responsible by providing a variety of parenting classes and family involvement activities. She felt that the interaction a parent has with the child at home is linked with how the child responds to adults and his peers at school, so it would be helpful for the school and home be consistent in modifying a child's behavior.

She also stated that;

"Maybe parents would have a more productive link with the schools if they felt that they were working together for the good of the whole child."

Parents had the understanding that the home is responsible for making sure children have their school materials, such as pencils and notebooks.

Another parent said,

"Parents should give their children more than school supplies; parents should also supply children with emotional support. When a parent is emotionally missing in their children's education, their children feel lost. They do not care about their schoolwork because they feel that no one at home cares. You can't teach a child who doesn't have the desire to learn; that is something that should be reinforced at home."

Do parents realize how important this emotional link with their children's educational process is? Do they need support and training in the basic daily needs of a child?

Schools take for granted that parents are making sure children are getting enough rest at night and are well fed. Parents felt that they should be doing such things, as well as keeping children safe by knowing where they are and monitoring their friends, but this does not always happen.

Child experts have suspected that a child's academic failures are most times symptoms of other problems.

One parent summed it up by commenting,

"Academic success starts at home, and then it flows with them through school. If parents set the standards from day one, the student will know what the expectations are. When a student fails, the parents, principal, and teacher need to take a close look to see why this happened and what can be done to get the child on the right track or in the right school."

Another observation was that parents who are not involved with their children's education—for example, parents who miss parent-teacher conferences multiple times without a valid reason—should be charged fees, and the money should be given to the school to help with programs.

The parent who made this observation commented,

"If all stakeholders were involved, it would allow for all thoughts, ideas, suggestions, possible problems, and solutions to be utilized in bringing up a successful child. Everyone who has contact with a child shares in the responsibility. If the child fails, we've all had a hand in the failure. Parents, especially, should know if their child is successful at school, and if the child is not learning, then they should do whatever is needed to improve the child's learning situation at home and at school. Parents should never stop being held responsible for their children's educational progress."

A high school principal and parent shared that he has witnessed parents giving up responsibility of their high school children. They start to decrease responsibility in middle school, he said. In contrast, during the elementary years they feel that "this is my baby," so they sometimes hold themselves more responsible than they hold the school. His perspective was,

"Whether or not parents feel responsible has a lot to do with parents feeling that children are more independent in high school. They may feel this way because they are tired from the challenges that come with having adolescent children. I have found that when a male child reaches ten to twelve years of age, single mothers feel that they need more help controlling him and will hold the school more responsible for the academic and social behavior of the child."

Another parent said that she felt responsible for her child not finishing high school because she did not finish. She is fifty-seven years old and is currently enrolled in an adult high school, attempting to earn a diploma. She is one of six girls raised by a single mom. She shared that her mother did not push education on her children. She was okay as long as they made a passing grade of a "D".

She also shared that her mother just wanted them out of school; she did not care if they finished high school because she knew that she could not send them to college.

"My mother felt that her responsibility was to feed the family; she did this by working two jobs. She did not get her high school diploma, but she did a good job raising us without an education. We never went to jail or did drugs. She taught us morals, values, and ethics. We were taught how to talk to adults, how to treat people, and how to be polite.

The mothers in the neighborhood felt that it was their responsibility to educate the girls by teaching us things like how to set the table, sew, and knit. My family let the children make their own decisions about education. I hold myself responsible for getting pregnant and quitting school in the tenth grade."

This parent also shared that she had three children. One of her children did not finish high school, and he stayed in trouble. She said it was hard to encourage him to finish school because he knew that she didn't finish.

"When I decided to go back to school to get my diploma, my son came back with me, and I am so proud of him. We both are at home, trying to do homework and asking each other questions. Sometimes my other children, his brother and sister, help us.

I feel that my going back to school has had a positive effect on my children, just like my quitting school had a negative effect on them. I would also like to think that my example to go back to school at my age is responsible for encouraging my son to value education now, while he is still young."

Another perspective of parents was that parents sometimes hold the child's friends responsible. They find ways to blame their child's bad social behavior on his friends.

One father of a teenager said that he has heard parents say,

"'If he wasn't hanging with that bad boy in his school, he wouldn't do the things he does.' The truth of the matter is that it is the responsibility of the parents to train their child how to choose the right friends. This is a part of his social development."

The parent of a four-year-old girl who will start school in the next year felt there is a huge disconnection between the family and the school, and this may be because the family unit does not seem to be an important part of society anymore.

He said,

"Some parents look at the school as a daycare and a way to get their children out of their hair. Kids are on their own to try to figure out and navigate their way through the education system and sometimes even life."

Another parent's viewpoint concerning being responsible was,

"For the most part, if parents are missing out on their kid's education, the parent is to blame. Schools give parents many opportunities to play an active role; parents too often don't make it a priority.

I personally feel that it is a shared responsibility between parents and the school and community. The school has a job to do, but parents should be their backup; that means turning off the television and cell phones and working together with the child. It also takes the full community supporting the success of the child."

Having discussions with parents concerning their children's education was an interesting journey. As I spoke with the parents, I began to categorize their comments. I then used the different categories to create a summary of our discussions.

15   Summing Up the Discussions

Missing Link? was brought to a close by summing up the discussions I had with parents. It is my hope that this type of open dialogue with parents will not end. I felt that it was important that parents were not restricted or influenced in the way they responded during our conversations.

My desire was to gain the true perspectives of parents concerning the educational process of their children, with emphasis on their role in the process. By doing so, child-care providers would get a better understanding of how to connect with parents. Many questions developed from the conversations, and I found that getting parents to share how they felt by discussing the questions that emerged proved a valuable way for them to communicate their perspectives. Common responses to the questions were put into categories; the categories were used to make summations about the conversations.

As a result, parents of different social and economic status have shared and can continue to learn from each other's experiences. Several conclusions can be gleaned by summing up the overall perspectives that parents shared.

From the discussions, we find that parents need to be empowered, and to do so they need to be informed. They need to be included and play an active, effective role in the educational process of their children. This may mean providing resources and the support parents need, such as time-management and parenting classes, which will ensure that parents are equipped with necessary tools.

Parents will need to be at the school, playing an active role in their child's education, in order to guarantee that all children receive what they need to be successful, academically and socially. Communication is the key.

Parents also felt they need to find ways that will make their presence in the schools a positive experience because when all stakeholders link together, a strong chain of success is formed for the child. The community, home, church, and school should form a supportive chain that will support children and keep them from being bound by failure. To be successful, none of the links of this chain can be missing.

Weak links also need to be identified and strengthened. Another perspective was to hold themselves more accountable. Parents cannot let life challenges and their personal endeavors keep them from knowing what is going on with their children. They realized that they cannot always wait for schools to offer them the support system they need. Most parents determined that they would have to seek and request support.

Another factor concerning how parent influence their children was shared. It was identified that how parents perceive ideals—"We are what we think"; "We accomplish what we know we can"; "Education is important and should be given priority"; and many more personal beliefs—motivate how their children feel and may set the groundwork for their success and failure in school.

Parents strongly expressed that school teachers and administrators should not assume that parents do not care about their child's education because they are low-income. Support systems and conversations need to happen for parents of all ethnic and social economic stations in life.

As I spoke with parents of different cultural and economic backgrounds, they all expressed that at times there are life challenges that prevent them from giving their children's education their full attention. Parents of higher economic status are sometimes more invested in their children's education and therefore are more involved with monitoring their investment by making sure their children are being educated in the best possible way.

Parents who are less invested and overwhelmed with everyday survival felt that if their children are fed and have clothes to wear to school that the school should appreciate their efforts, and if the children do not perform in school, it is on the teachers and the school to support them.

Until educators truly communicate and understand the perspectives of parents, they will continue to make the determination that parents are the missing link—but are they?

Most all of the parents I spoke with felt that parents were missing in the educational process of their children in some way. Some parents were satisfied with their roles but thought that because they defined their roles differently from the school system that the school did not feel they were doing enough. The parents deemed that they were doing all that they could.

A small number of parents blamed themselves for not being truly linked or even caring enough to be linked to their children's education. They felt they had enough to worry about just getting through day-to-day concerns and survival.

"I no longer have a … us-against-them mentality," said one parent, "and I see the importance that all the links have in supporting our children's education. When one link is weak or missing, we all pay the price because if children are unsuccessful, they will become a burden on their parents and society."

Parents also shared that having the discussions helped them reflect on their involvement in their children's education and the importance of staying connected with their overall academic and social development. After our discussions, parents expressed that they were very thankful for the chance to talk openly about how they felt. Some of them revealed that the discussions helped them to reevaluate whether or not they were linked to the educational process of their children.

It is my desire that parents will know that it is okay to ask questions and have conversations with other parents and with those educating their children. There is much more to be learned from listening to the perspectives of parents.

The interview questions were designed to encourage and motivate conversations with parents. The responses to the questions became the discussion topics for the chapters of the book *Missing Link?* **No methodical circumstances were used; however,** I created **a method to share parent responses in an organized and accurate manner for the reader. Parent quotes were not transcribed. I took notes, redirected questions, and used open-ended questioning to glean parent perspectives.**

Having discussions with parents concerning their children's education was an interesting journey. Many studies show that parents who stay connected to the educational process are helping to nurture the cognitive development of their children. Children with involved parents are motivated to achieve.

Part 5

Nurturing the Whole Child

Part 5

Nurturing the Whole Child

An article by Kim Austin, American Rose Society (ARS) consulting rosarian, quoted an English poet Alfred Austin, who wrote,

"The glory of gardening: hands in the dirt, head in the sun, heart with nature, to nurture a garden is to feed not just the body, but the soul."

She felt that this poem caused her to ponder, "Why do I grow roses? Why do I garden at all when it requires blood, sweat, and tears?"

Like the rosarian Kim Austin, caring for children may cause caregivers to ponder if caring for someone else's children is worth the effort. Fortunately, many fight through it and continue to put the passion they have for children in the forefront. Today, most children spend Monday through Friday in a child-care facility as parents work to provide for them.

My experience supporting and training child-care workers and parents has caused me to have admiration for their passion, dedication, and sacrifice. I feel that they are sometimes on what I call the battlefield for children—on the battlefield, fighting for the social, emotional, and academic success of children. As a society, we have fought for a lot of things—the right to bear arms, the right for free speech, and the freedom to choose. I am talking, however, about fighting for the right children have to be healthy and whole.

Children have the right to be nurtured and given everything they need to be successful in life. When children are unmanageable, confused, and unmotivated, somehow we blame them. Children need a weapon against things that can defeat them. The most powerful weapons in this battle are the adults in their lives, most importantly the caregivers and parents. *Parent* refers to anyone legally responsible for the child (e.g., grandparent, aunt, or guardian). Of course, children need other weapons and strategies, such as community, church, and government, to be on the battlefield.

Normally, when we hear the phrase "mind, body, and spirit," it describes the being of an adult. It is important to remember, however, that children are little human beings. Nurturing the whole child takes into consideration his or her mind, body and spirit; this embraces the social, emotional, and cognitive health of the child.

16   Mind

Like flowers in a garden, children flourish outdoors. Children love to be out in the sun, fresh air, wind, and rain. If they could, they would take off all of their clothes and dance, jump, and run around naked, eating dirt. They would be happy to play in the mud and splash in puddles. This activity supports the child's free will.

Merriam-Webster defines the mind as "the intellectual or rational faculty in man, the understanding; the intellect; the power that conceives, judges, or reasons; also the entire nature; the soul often distinction from all the body. The state at any given time of the faculties of thinking, willing, choosing, and like, psychical activity or state, choice, inclination, liking, intent and will."

Mental-health experts state that the mind of a child with good mental health will think clearly, develop socially and cognitively, and build self-esteem and self-regulation.

When we look at a flower garden, it is evident by the beauty of the flowers that experts take care of it. The mental well-being of children is not always as obvious. In order to ensure that a child's mind is developing properly, caregivers need to look to the experts.

According to mental-health experts, a child's caregivers should be just as diligent in helping to prevent mental health issues as they are in preventing physical illnesses and injuries. It is vital that mental-health needs are identified at an early age.

The website Mental Health America: Children's Mental Health Matters, suggests that the following are basic needs to ensure children's good mental health:

- Give unconditional love.

- Nurture a child's confidence and self-esteem.

- Encourage children to play.

- Enroll children in an after-school activity.

- Provide a safe and secure environment.

- Give appropriate guidance and discipline when necessary.

- Communicate.

- Get help if there is a concern about a child's mental health

For more information on identifying mental health issues in children and what parents and teachers can do, go to the Mental Health America website at www. mentalhealthamerica.net.

17   Body

Webster's Dictionary defines a person as "a human being frequently in composition; as anybody, nobody, and somebody. As distinguished from the spirit, or vital principle; the physical person." A child's body goes through many transitional stages on the journey to adulthood. It is no accident that child-care facilities and schools provide nutritionally balanced meals for children. As a school principal, it was my responsibility to monitor what was being served to the children in the cafeteria.

I had occasion to meet with the nutritionist to discuss a complaint by the children that the cafeteria did not offer enough variety. During the conversation, I learned why certain items and not others were offered (possible allergies, for example) and that the meals were balanced to ensure the nutritional needs of all children were met (it's the law).

Plants need nourishment to grow to their full potential, beauty, and ability to reproduce. Proper nourishment is vital to the growth and well-being of children as well. What happens when flowers don't get enough water or the soil does not contain enough nutrients? The leaves can wither, and blooms will fall off; the flowers are not as beautiful and can even die.

The effect of malnutrition on children has been well documented. When a woman is pregnant, she must receive the proper nourishment for herself and the child.

If the mother is malnourished, then the child she is carrying will be malnourished—and this can have devastating and lasting effects on the child.

Studies show that malnourishment can impede social, emotional, and cognitive development and affect the reproductive and productive health of the child into school-age and adulthood. An article by Sagan and Druyan (1994) reveals that if children are not well nourished during their first years of life, their ill health will affect their ability to learn, think, and communicate. The article also stated that when the body doesn't get enough food, it has to make a decision about how to invest the limited nourishment available. Survival will come first, growth is second, and learning last.

Just as plants can be overwatered, children can overeat. Experts define malnutrition as a condition that results from eating a diet that does not have enough or *has too many* nutrients. Not enough nutrients is called "undernutrition"; too much is called "over nutrition." If undernutrition occurs during pregnancy or before age two, the lack proper nurturance could cause permanent underdeveloped physical and mental development, a balanced nutritional foundation is needed to nurture the child's body to its full potential.

18   Spirit

I have included the sections on mind, body, and spirit to encourage readers of *Nurture* to see children as little human beings who are solely dependent on the adults in their lives as they develop into the persons they will become.

These little human being have to learn how to manage the different aspects of life. It is inevitable that they understand moral and ethical behavior.

Beginning at a young age children who learn to pray began to learn about having a relationship with God. Punishment should not be the premise behind why they thrive to be a decent person. Children should be taught how to connect with their emotional selves through having a good spirit. The most heartbreaking vision is a child with a sad or broken spirit.

I shared earlier that children think about suicide at young ages. As adults, we should hold ourselves morally responsible for the spiritual well-being of children. The relationships that children have with adults can strengthen or break their spirits. You may recall that children are molded by the relationships they have with the adults in their lives. It is for this reason that children's caregivers should resist viewing children as little things that should be played with and then set aside when the caregivers are too tired or don't want to be bothered. They should know that children are our first and most important priority.

Merriam-Webster defines the spirit of a person as the rational and immortal part of humans—that part of humans that enables them to think and the emotional part of human nature. It is the seat of feeling distinct from intellect; the vehicle of individual personal existence; the surviving entity.

A broken spirit is hard to mend. As a child, I experienced having a broken spirit.

When My Spirit Was Broken

I was a very shy child, living with eight siblings and my parents. From an early age, I always wanted to make my mother proud of me. I wanted to grow up to be someone who would make a difference in the world. When I started school, I remember being very upset when my mother left me there with people I did not know. My next memory of school is when I was in the fourth grade; I had a strong desire to be in Ms. Smith's fifth-grade class. I did all my work in the fourth grade, even homework. The teacher seemed to be pleased with me until the last day of school, when she told me that I would not be passed to the fifth grade and had to repeat the fourth grade.

I cried and begged her to let me pass. I cried so long and hard that she finally said that if I went to summer school and received A's and B's that she would pass me. She also gave me her phone number. I stopped crying and went home, but my heart was still broken because I had to face my family.

That summer I went to school and worked very hard. Throughout the summer I called my fourth grade teacher, wanting to tell her how hard I was working and that

I was making good grades. Whenever I called her, however, the person who answered the phone said that she was in Florida. I don't remember doing anything else that summer except schoolwork and calling my teacher. As a result of my hard work, I earned all "A's" and one "B".

At the start of the new school year, I was excited to show her my report card so that I could be promoted to Ms. Smith's fifth-grade class. The first day of school I went up to my fourth-grade teacher with a big smile on my face and handed her my report card; I waited for her response. She looked at me and said. "This is good, but you can't go to Ms. Smith's class. You are still in the fourth grade." She then reached in her desk and handed me a souvenir soap dish from Florida, saying, "This is for you."

After that, I experienced a heavy feeling that I cannot explain. My spirit was broken. I did not care about school anymore. I believe that this is part of the reason for the passion I have to ensure that all children receive the nurturing they need. I carried this heaviness all the way to high school. In my senior year in high school, I became pregnant and gave birth to a little girl.

As I held my daughter in my arms, I realized that my life had changed—now I was responsible for another life. As I watched her grow from an infant to a toddler, a realization came over me that this little person needed more from me than food and clothing. I would need to keep her safe as she explored the world around her.

No one told me how to do that as my daughter went through each stage—walking, talking, and entering school.

I did not know to put her in preschool, so her first day of school was kindergarten. I really did not want to leave her there; her first day was harder on me than it was on her. I felt that I had no control over what would happen to her throughout the day. She was becoming a part of the world that would influence her social and emotional development. I was not sure what social and emotional development meant or how to protect her from any damage that she could possibly obtain from interacting with adults and peers.

It seemed that my daughter became a teenage overnight, and I knew she would leave for college soon. I always wanted to give her something she could take with her—my faith. She had my love, and I wanted her to know that no matter what happened to her in life, she could always look to God to keep her spirit strong. When children are exposed to love, security, and faith, their souls are cared for. A cared-for soul is happy, and the happy soul of a child is one that can conceive of who he or she is, be resilient, and find his or her place in this world.

Part 6

Creating Nurturing Environments

Part 6

Creating Nurturing Environments

During a visit to a local garden nursery, I observed an environment that was conducive to the growth of healthy plants. The caregivers were trained, and they seemed to have a passion for what they were doing. The plants were nurtured in a way that was different for each variety. In the same way, when one enters a preschool, the environment should demonstrate that children are socially, emotionally, and cognitively nurtured.

A nurturing home is equally important. According to the National Center for Children in Poverty (www.nccp.org), negative early experiences, such as poverty, can impair children's mental health and affect cognitive, social, and emotional development. However, because a significant percentage of children spend a great deal of their waking hours in child-care facilities, it is vital to their developmental health that these environments are nurturing as well.

According to "America's Children in Brief: Key National Indicators of Well-Being, 2015" (at childstats.gov, an online forum on child and family statistics), in 2011, 49 percent of children ages birth to four years old with employed mothers were primarily cared for by a relative; 24 percent spent most of their time in a child-care facility; and 13 percent were cared for by a non-relative in a home environment, such as with a nanny or babysitter.

Among children in families in poverty in 2011, 18 percent were in child-care facilities, and 19 percent were with a relative who was not their mother, father, or grandparent. By comparison, a greater percentage of children in families at or above the poverty level were in child-care facilities (26 percent), and only 4 percent were cared for by other relatives. In 2012, about 62 percent of children ages three to six and not in kindergarten were in child-care facilities.

Although many studies show no conclusive evidence that child-care facilities on average are either better or worse for the development of children than being cared for by parents. Research does show that consistent, developmentally sound nurturing and supportive care has a positive effect on children and their parents. Most important, high-quality child care is the component that ensures the healthy social, emotional, and cognitive development of children. To find more on quality early learning education and child care, go to naeyc.org.

Low-income children who attend intensive, nurturing, high-quality early education programs have greater school success, higher graduation rates, lower levels of juvenile crime, decreased need for special education services, and lower teenage pregnancy rates than their peers (F. A. Campbell 2000).

As allotted to earlier The National Center for Injury Prevention and Control (CDC) document stated that because children experience their world through the relationships and interactions they have with adults, it is important for these relationships to be safe, stable, and nurturing. These three qualities also apply to the environment to which children are exposed a daily basis because it makes a difference for children as they grow and develop.

An article by Linda Dusenbury, PhD, on the Education World website shared that children need to feel safe in order to learn. "One of the most important things teachers can do to promote learning is to create classroom environments where students feel safe."

Communication, collaboration, and personal sacrifice for the good of children will have to take place in order to create nurturing environments in preschools.

19 Working Together to Creating a Nurturing Environment for Children

To create a nurturing preschool environment, every adult—teachers (and co-teachers), classroom assistants, lead teachers, directors (supervisors, administration) and parents—must be committed to it. My personal observations of the interaction between teachers and administration revealed that they must work together to make a nurturing environment for children a reality.

- A nurturing environment for children cannot be burdened with adult conflict.
- A nurturing environment for children cannot consist of bad attitudes between adults.

There is an old saying, "It takes a village to raise a child," yet most people say that the village no longer exists. Who are we talking about when we say "village" today? The village is different from past interpretations. Today, the adults in the child-care facilities are a large part of the village. This means all must focus on the needs of children because child-care workers are literally a part of raising someone else's children.

Children watch, learn, and model what they see adults doing. Adult interactions with each other must be consistent with the social and emotional lessons that the children in their care are expected to master. The relationship that the adults have with each other is a part of the children's reality. The children see how the adults interact with each other, and they hear what the adults say about each other.

Communication

When children do not see the correct modeling of behavior and are witness to outbursts and quarreling among the adults, a feeling of insecurity and distrust can develop. Child-care experts have long suggested that in order for children to thrive they have to feel secure and safe.

Co-teachers can have a wonderful experience, when planning and communication are in place. This can be done by establishing rapport with each other. During my many visits to child-care facilities, I have witnessed what happens when communication does not take place between co-teachers. There is an uncomfortable relationship between them and the children, in turn, feel uncomfortable. The daily activities do not flow, which causes escalated discipline issues.

A positive relationship between co-teachers can be created by planning ahead. This means communicating to minimize misunderstandings and determining each other's teaching and classroom-management styles and using them to create a cohesive, stable classroom. Knowing each other's strengths and weaknesses can help develop a positive rapport and resolve problems before they escalate. The key is to discuss and plan in advance to avoid getting into a heated discussion in front of the children.

Collaboration

When the adults collaborate, they can use their personal styles to complement each other, which will create a nurturing environment for children. Child-care teachers and directors should have consistent expectations and should all be on the same page with regard to instruction, discipline, and parent communication. Decisions that are made for the facility should involve collaboration with all, not done in isolation. Suggestions for collaborating with parents include the following:

- Involve parents with the development of the school's discipline policy.
- Offer parent-support workshops (e.g., on discipline and parenting).
- Create parent groups similar to the PTO in elementary schools.

I observed one interaction between the supervisors and administrators of a child-care facility that caused me concern. They made a major decision about the rotation of the children—changing the length of time teachers spent with each age group—without involving the teachers. When this change was implemented, it was obvious that there was no commitment from the teachers, who felt that the decision prevented them from bonding with the children and their parents.

Administration, in this case, took my suggestion to take the issue back to the table and to invite input from the teachers. The result was a collaborated plan that had the commitment of all for the good of the children.

Personal Sacrifice

Nurturing children is one of the most important and unrecognized jobs in the world. Creating a nurturing environment will take personal sacrifice. Personal sacrifice means putting the needs of the children first.

- Be willing to overlook the imperfections of others and work together as a team.
- Be willing to recognize personal weaknesses.
- Be willing to sacrifice time for training that will increase the skills needed to nurture children.

Personal sacrifice also means that the caregiver puts aside negative reactions to what is happening in his or her personal life and maintains a positive attitude and demeanor for the children. This does not mean being a pretender, but it does mean doing whatever is necessary to make a sincere effort toward preventing social or emotional damage to the children with whom the caregiver interacts.

Caregivers should realize that they are an important part of the team, and without everyone's dedication, it is impossible to create a nurturing environment for children.

Conclusion

The passion I have for preventing developmental damage to young children moved me to pen *Nurture*. Personal observations in child-care facilities revealed that child-care workers, such as preschool teachers, understand the need for age-appropriate activities and learning strategies. However, connecting cognitive development with the social and emotional development of young children was unintentionally overlooked and misunderstood by most. This connection is crucial when young children transition through each stage of their development. Research shows that young children who are socially and emotionally stable learn, thrive, and grow up to have a more positive teenage experience.

Children's differences come from genetics and situations to which they are exposed, socially, emotionally, and cognitively. As they grow and develop, whatever they are exposed to becomes the ground that nurtures or depletes them. Child-care professionals have an obligation to obtain expertise in all areas of child development. Children are not only our product but the future of this world. As Part 1 noted, just as gardeners seek the expertise of rosarians to obtain the skills necessary to successfully grow roses, we, as children's caregivers, must be dedicated to obtaining the knowledge of experts in the field of child development.

Emotional development involves many learned behaviors, as revealed in Part 2 of this book. Human beings grow from infancy to toddlers; toddlers grow to school age. How healthily they develop depends upon how knowledgeable (or deficient) their caregivers (parents, guardians, child-care providers, teachers) are. This is important because children develop self-regulation and other coping skills by modeling the adults with whom they interact. For this reason, positive relationships are vital.

Studies in the three areas of child development also revealed that children develop cognitively as they development socially and emotionally and that their social and emotional needs play a role in the learning (cognitive) process.

Part 3 delved briefly into brain research and other studies pertaining to how the brain develops from infancy to school age. Information about brain research indicates that children are ready to learn specific cognitive skills at different ages and levels of mental development. Therefore, children's caregivers must provide activities that are precise and age-appropriate and that accommodate the level at which children are mentally ready to learn.

Parents are brought into the picture in Part 4, as the perspectives on the educational process of their children are investigated. Interviews with parents set the groundwork for conversations around this issue. The intention was not to provide answers to any question but to stimulate awareness to the type of support parents may need as they endeavor to nurture and connect to their children's educational experiences. The perspectives of parents showed that one key way to nurture this connection was effective communication. To communicate effectively, dialogue cannot be blaming; on the contrary, it should be open, trusting, and welcoming.

Part 5 reminded the reader that children are little human beings with minds, bodies, and spirits. Children need more than food for their bodies; their minds also need nourishment that encourages the body to develop in a healthy way. Nourishment in the form of unconditional love produces a child with a loving, secure spirit.

In the same way that flowers flourish when properly nurtured, studies show that nurturing school and home environments have a positive effect on children. Part 6 covered why and how to create nurturing environments for young children. Suggestions were provided for children's caregivers that encouraged communication, collaboration, and unconditional love. Because children get cues from the adults in their lives, caregivers must be mindful of their relationships and interactions with each other as well.

In addition, Part 6 gave recognition to the personal sacrifice one must be willing to make when caring for children. Every adult who has accepted this important responsibility must hold himself or herself accountable for the emotional, social, and cognitive health of the children in his or her care. It is my desire that *Nurture* will provide insight into a way that is precise and beneficial in this important undertaking.

About the Author

Mattie Lee Solomon, PhD, for over 20 years Dr. Solomon has been involved in the education of countless children and adults, including having worked as a teacher and a school principal. Dr. Solomon's work as a university professor and department chair afforded her the opportunity to develop and enhance Early Childhood Education programs.

Dr. Solomon is a member of the National Association for the Education of Young Children (NAEYC) and serves on the board of the Indiana Association for the Education of Young Children (IAEYC), where she is the chair of professional development.

Her abundance of experience with children and parents motivated her to pen her first book, *Missing Link?*, which documents parents' perspectives concerning the education of their children. Dr. Solomon's second book, *What Did Your Parent Do to You*, reveals true stories that open windows to how childhood experiences influence the journeys people take through life, as well as how they parent.

Her experience as a presenter, trainer, and supporter of child-care workers and providers motivated her to pen *Disciplining Someone Else's Children (A Guide for Child Care Providers)*, which is a fact-based guide to discipline for preschool children. Her book *Nurture* comes from the desire to continue to support and connect the social, emotional, and cognitive development of children.

Dr. Solomon earned a K–12 business education degree from the University of Indianapolis; a master's degree in K–12 educational administration from Ball State University, Muncie, Indiana; and a PhD in the philosophy of education from Indiana State University, Terra Haute, Indiana.

References

American Academy of Pediatrics, https://www.aap.org, accessed 2016

America's Children in Brief: Key National Indicators of Well-Being, www.Childstats. gov/americaschildren, 2015

Bell, M. & Wolfe, C. (2004). Emotion and Cognition: An Intricately Bound Developmental Process in Child Development 75 (2): 36670 Feb. 2004.

Birch, S., & Ladd, G. Interpersonal Relationship in the School Environment & Children's Early School Adjustment: The Role of Teachers & Peers, (1996).

Campbell, F. A., Early Learning Later Success: The Abecedarian Study, http://fpg. unc.edu/resouce/early-learning-later-success-abecedarian-study Process Child Development, (2000). Vol. 75 No. 2, 366–70.

Child Action: The Importance of Play, www.childaction.org/families/publications/ docs/guidance/handout13-the_importance_of_play.pdf, accessed 2016

Cherry, Kendra *"What is Art Therapy"*, www.verywell.com-2795755 (2016): Essentials for Childhood Framework: Steps to Create Safe, Stable, Nurturing Relationship and Environment for Children, The National Center for Injury Prevention & Control www.cdcgov/violenceprevention/pdf/ essentials_for_childhood_framework.pdf, August 2014 (p.7)

Dusenbury, Linda PhD, *"Creating a Safe Classroom Environment"* Education World article, educationworld.com/a_curri/creating-safe-classroomenviroment-climates.shtml accessed 2016

Facts for Life, *"Child Development & Early Learning Facts"*, 4th edition, www. factsforlifeglobal.org/03/1.html accessed 2016

Gable, Sara *"Nature, Nurture and Early Brain Development"* article 30, May 3, 2008, www.classbrain.com

Galinsky, Ellen *"Mind in the Making, Seven Essential Life Skills Every Child Needs"*, 1st edition, pp 321–322. (2010)

Kushnir, Tamar, *"Learning about How Children Learn,"* Cornell University, www. human.cornell.edu/nd/outreach/upload/learning-about-how-children-learn-Kushnir, (2009).

Laughlin, Lynda *"Who's Minding the Kids?"* www.census.gov/prod/2013pubs/ page70-135, (April 2013)

Mental Health America, www.metalhealthamerica.net, (2016)

The National Association for the Education of Young Children, www.Naeyc.org/
DAP, Accessed 2016

Perry, Bruce MD, PhD *"How Children Learn Language"* Early Childhood Today,
scholastic.com/teachers/article/how-young-children-learn-langauage (2016)

Sagan, C., A. Druyan *"Literacy the Path to a More Prosperous Less Dangerous
America" Parade* magazine, March 6, 1994.

Solomon, Mattie Lee, *"Disciplining Someone Else's Children "*, iUniverse (2015).

Solomon, Mattie Lee, *"What Did Your Parents Do to You"*, iUniverse (2014).

Solomon, Mattie Lee, *Missing Link?*, iUniverse. (2011).

The American Rose Society (ARS), www.rose.org, accessed 2016

The National Center for Injury Prevention (CDC) www.cdc.gov/violenceprevention.
Accessed 2016

The National Association for the Education of Young Children (NAEYC), www.
naeyc.org accessed 2016

The Human Memory www.human-memory.net/brain neurons.html. (2010),

Winfrey, Oprah *"What I Know for Sure"*, Flatiron Books (September, 2014).

Printed in the United States
By Bookmasters